1932
HOPI AND NAVAJO
NATIVE AMERICAN CENSUS
WITH BIRTH & DEATH ROLLS
(1930 - 1932)
VOLUME 2 - NAVAJO

TRANSCRIBED BY
JEFF BOWEN

NATIVE STUDY
Gallipolis, Ohio
USA

Copyright © 2013
by Jeff Bowen

ALL RIGHTS RESERVED
No part of this publication may be reproduced
or used in any form or manner whatsoever
without previous written permission from the
copyright holder or publisher.

Originally published:
Baltimore, Maryland
2013

Reprinted by:

Native Study LLC
Gallipolis, OH
www.nativestudy.com
2020

Library of Congress Control Number: 2020916727

ISBN: 978-1-64968-056-3

Made in the United States of America.

Other Books and Series by Jeff Bowen

1901-1907 Native American Census Seneca, Eastern Shawnee, Miami, Modoc, Ottawa, Peoria, Quapaw, and Wyandotte Indians (Under Seneca School, Indian Territory)

1932 Census of The Standing Rock Sioux Reservation with Births And Deaths 1924-1932

Census of The Blackfeet, Montana, 1897- 1901 Expanded Edition

Eastern Cherokee by Blood, 1906-1910, Volumes I thru XIII

Choctaw of Mississippi Indian Census 1929-1932 with Births and Deaths 1924-1931 Volume I

Choctaw of Mississippi Indian Census 1933, 1934 & 1937, Supplemental Rolls to 1934 & 1935 with Births and Deaths 1932-1938, and Marriages 1936-1938 Volume II

Eastern Cherokee Census Cherokee, North Carolina 1930-1939 Census 1930-1931 with Births And Deaths 1924-1931 Taken By Agent L. W. Page Volume I

Eastern Cherokee Census Cherokee, North Carolina 1930-1939 Census 1932-1933 with Births And Deaths 1930-1932 Taken By Agent R. L. Spalsbury Volume II

Eastern Cherokee Census Cherokee, North Carolina 1930-1939 Census 1934-1937 with Births and Deaths 1925-1938 and Marriages 1936 & 1938 Taken by Agents R. L. Spalsbury And Harold W. Foght Volume III

Seminole of Florida Indian Census, 1930-1940 with Birth and Death Records, 1930-1938

Texas Cherokees 1820-1839 A Document For Litigation 1921

Choctaw By Blood Enrollment Cards 1898-1914 Volumes I thru XVII

Starr Roll 1894 (Cherokee Payment Rolls) Districts: Canadian, Cooweescoowee, and Delaware Volume One

Starr Roll 1894 (Cherokee Payment Rolls) Districts: Flint, Going Snake, and Illinois Volume Two

Starr Roll 1894 (Cherokee Payment Rolls) Districts: Saline, Sequoyah, and Tahlequah; Including Orphan Roll Volume Three

Other Books and Series by Jeff Bowen

Cherokee Intruder Cases Dockets of Hearings 1901-1909 Volumes I & II

Indian Wills, 1911-1921 Records of the Bureau of Indian Affairs Books One thru Seven;

Native American Wills & Probate Records 1911-1921

Turtle Mountain Reservation Chippewa Indians 1932 Census with Births & Deaths, 1924-1932

Chickasaw By Blood Enrollment Cards 1898-1914 Volume I thru V

Cherokee Descendants East An Index to the Guion Miller Applications Volume I
Cherokee Descendants West An Index to the Guion Miller Applications Volume II (A-M)
Cherokee Descendants West An Index to the Guion Miller Applications Volume III (N-Z)

Applications for Enrollment of Seminole Newborn Freedmen, Act of 1905

Eastern Cherokee Census, Cherokee, North Carolina, 1915-1922, Taken by Agent James E. Henderson   Volume I (1915-1916)
*   Volume II (1917-1918)*
*   Volume III (1919-1920)*
*   Volume IV (1921-1922)*

Complete Delaware Roll of 1898

Eastern Cherokee Census, Cherokee, North Carolina, 1923-1929, Taken by Agent James E. Henderson   Volume I (1923-1924)
*   Volume II (1925-1926)*
*   Volume III (1927-1929)*

Applications for Enrollment of Seminole Newborn Act of 1905 Volumes I & II

North Carolina Eastern Cherokee Indian Census 1898-1899, 1904, 1906, 1909-1912, 1914 Revised and Expanded Edition

1932 Hopi and Navajo Native American Census with Birth & Death Rolls (1925-1931) Volume 1 - Hopi

Visit our website at **www.nativestudy.com** to learn more about these and other books and series by Jeff Bowen

This series is dedicated to the
Navajo and Hopi people.

TABLE OF CONTENTS

Introduction……………………………….vii

Census Instructions……………………..ix

1932 Navajo Indian Census……………..1

Live Births

      1929-1930……………………………..61
      1930-1931……………………………..64

Deaths

      1930-1931………………….…..…67

      Supplemental Death Report……69

Index…………………………..………….71

INTRODUCTION

This census was originally transcribed by this author in April 1997. The census was placed in two volumes because there was such a large difference involving the structure of yearly separations, as is evident from the table of contents for each volume. This work was obtained from National Archives microfilm M-595, Roll 192.

The Hopi Indians, are a divisional group of the Pueblo peoples from the Southwest cultural area. Living in northeastern Arizona they usually lived near high mesas or flat-topped hills with steep sides where they formed pueblos, small communities or villages that were self-governed.

Hopi people are known as diligent agriculturists as well as very talented artisans. The Hopi religion emphasizes worship of the forces of nature, and has many different ceremonies intended to invoke supernatural powers. A few of the more important Hopi religious ceremonies include: the Kachina Fertility mysteries as well as the Midsummer and Midwinter rituals of Sun and Fire worship. The most intense ceremony performed and celebrated by the Hopi people is the Snake dance which is staged every two years. They also practice the Kachina Dance as well as the Flute ceremony. They feel their people have a roll as caretakers of the earth.

As with most Native cultures the Hopi people have watched their culture change with the modernization of American life and population increase. From the 2010 publication, *Indian Nations of North America*, it states "Hopi people refer to their ancestors as Hisatsinom ("People of Long Ago"), while archaeologists refer to them as Anasazi or San Juan basketmakers. They formed small settlements in a region stretching from the Grand Canyon to Toko'navi (Navajo Mountain) in present-day Utah, eastward to the Lukachukai Mountains near the New Mexico-Arizona border, and south to the Mogollon Rim. Small masonry villages were built between 900 and 1100, but a severe, long-lasting drought forced the abandonment of 36 of the 47 mesa-top villages. Following the drought, the 11 remaining villages grew in size, and three more were developed. Thus, the modern-day Hopi have lived in the Black Mesa region of the Colorado Plateau for nearly 1,000 years. The Hopi village of Old Oraibi is considered one of the oldest continuously occupied cities in the United States.

"The Spanish visited the region several times between 1540 and the Pueblo Revolt in 1680. During the revolt, the Hopi moved many of their villages to mesa tops for defensive purposes and sheltered refugees from other pueblos."[1]

"The Hopi currently live in 13 villages on three thin mesas projecting south from Black Mesa and to the west along Moencopi Wash. Their homeland is called Tutsqua. Every village is relatively autonomous, but only one has adopted a constitution and established a westernized government--the 11 other villages operate with some degree of adherence to the traditional Hopi form of governance. Oraibi remains traditional."[2]

---

[1] National Geographic Indian Nations of North America p. 213-214.
[2] National Geographic Indian Nations of North America p. 214.

INTRODUCTION

The Navajo, also spelled Navaho, Indians of the Southwest also live on reservations in northeastern Arizona, while parts adjoin to both New Mexico and Utah. They originally called themselves Tinneh or the People, but with time they would be called Apache and Navajo by people they came in contact with. Their dialects were from the same Athapaskan decent. Their religion was simply founded on overseeing nature and healing the sick. Eventually, "Like any people spread out over a vast and variable landscape, they gradually splintered into distinct groups, which the Spaniards began to distinguish with separate names."[3] "Spread out along the northern borders of New Mexico and Arizona were the Apaches de Nabajo--later shorten to Navajo--who developed a far different way of life than the other groups."[4] In time they would become so different that they would identify themselves as the, Dine', The People. During the early times they began to live where the very ancient Anasazi lived. The Navajo became herdsmen, raising sheep and horses; Navajo women became weavers of the finest blankets. "In times of want, weaving often kept Navajo families alive. Woman sheared the sheep, and spun and dyed the wool, obtaining the soft hues from wild plants."[5]

Today the Navajo Reservation is the largest reservation in the United States; in fact, it is larger than the state of West Virginia.

"The tribe is a member of the Eight Northern Indian Pueblos Council, a nonprofit organization that provides community-based services to Nambė, Taos, Picuris, Ohkay Owingeh, Santa Clara, San Ildefonso, Pojoaque, and Tesuque Pueblos. The tribal economy is supported in large part from the tribe's agricultural enterprises."[6]

This two volume set contains a wealth of genealogical information that reveals the name, age at last birthday, marital status, degree of blood, relationship to Head of family, and in the case of the Hopi, the village the family was living at during the time of the census. The Birth and Death Rolls also contain valuable information like birth and death dates, the mother's and father's degree of blood, and in most cases the cause of death.

Jeff Bowen
Gallipolis, Ohio
NativeStudy.com

---

[3] The American Indians, People of The Desert p. 142.
[4] The American Indians, People of The Desert p. 142-145
[5] The American Indians, People of The Desert p. 166.
[6] Indian Nations of North America p. 224.

INSTRUCTIONS

(*A*) A separate roll is to be made of each reservation; also, of each *rancheria* or reserve, and a separate roll of Indians allotted on the public domain or homesteading. The roll is to be based on enrollment and not on residence.

(*B*) Persons are to be listed by families alphabetically; that is, not only by the first letter of the surname, but also by the second and subsequent letters when the first letter or letters are the same. For example: Ab*a*lon, Ab*b*ott, Ab*c*on, Ab*e*nd, Ab*i*ct; B*a*ll, B*e*ll, B*i*ll, B*o*ll, B*u*ll; ...etc. Families having the same surname are also to be listed in this way, e.g.; Brown, *A*nson; Brown, *B*ill; Brown, *C*harles; Brown, *D*avid. In the case of English translations of Indian names, such as John *Flying-Elk*, Flying-Elk is the surname and is to be listed under F. In such cases the first word of the translated Indian name determines the alphabetical position. The best way to accomplish this will be to write the names of each family group on a separate card; then, arrange the cards alphabetically and type the names therefrom onto the census roll.

Members of a family are to be listed in the following order: Head, first; wife, second; then children, whether sons or daughters, *in the order of their ages*; and lastly, all other relatives and persons living with the family who do not constitute another family group.

Annuity and per capita payment rolls are also to be prepared in the same manner.

(*C*) A family is composed of the following members:
1. Both parents and their unmarried children, if any, living with them; all other relatives and persons living with the family who do not constitute another family group.
2. Either parent and the unmarried children, if the other parent is dead; all other relatives and persons living with the family who do not constitute another family group.
3. A single person over 21 years of age, not living with a relative.

(*D*) For each person the following information is to be furnished:
1. NUMBER. – A number is to be assigned in serial order. Thus, the first person listed is to be numbered as "1," the second, as "2," and so on until the census is completed.
2. NAME. – If there are both an Indian and an English name, the allotment or annuity roll name is to be given. First, the last or surname; then, the given name in full. Ditto marks are to be used under the surname of the head for the surnames of the other members of one family.
3. SEX. – "M" for male; "F" for female.
4. AGE AT LAST BIRTHDAY. – Age in completed years at last birthday is to be shown. For infants under 1 year, age in completed months, expressed as twelfths of a year. Thus, 3 months as 3/12 yr.

INSTRUCTIONS

5. TRIBE. – Care is to be taken that tribe, not band or local name, is given. Thus, Ute tribe, not Pahvant, which is a band of Ute. Likewise, Hupa tribe, not Bear River, which is a local name for the members of the Hupa tribe living near Bear River.
6. DEGREE OF BLOOD. – "F" for full blood; "1/4+" for one-fourth or more Indian blood; "-1/4" for less than one fourth Indian blood.
7. MARITAL STATUS. – "S" for a single or unmarried person; "M" for a married person; and "W" for widowed of either sex.
8. RELATIONSHIP TO HEAD OF FAMILY. – The head, whether husband or father, widow or unmarried person of either sex, is to be designated as such. For the other members, the appropriate term which designates the particular relationship the person bears to the head is to be used.
9. RESIDENCE. –
    (a) At *jurisdiction* where enrolled: Yes or no. The term jurisdiction includes all reservations and public domain allotments under the agency.
    (b) *Or* at another jurisdiction. The name of the jurisdiction is to be given.
    (c) *Or* elsewhere:
        1. Post office: Both the proper name of the post office and the class by which it is known (city, town, village, etc.) are to be given. Thus, Lewiston, city.
        2. County.
        3. State.
10. WARD. – Yes or no. Wardship depends primarily upon the ownership of individual property held in trust or upon membership in a tribe living on a Federal reservation.

* 11. ALLOTMENT, ANNUITY, AND IDENTIFICATION NUMBERS. —"Al", for allotment; "An", for annuity; and "Id", for identification, before the appropriate number or numbers. All numbers are to be shown.

** 11. (KEY TO VARIOUS HOPI VILLAGES). – Each letter represents a different village, as follows:
A - Tewa
B - Sitchumnovi
C - Walpi
D - Mashongnovi

INSTRUCTIONS

E - Chepaulovi
F - Chimopovy
G - Oraibi
H - Bacabi
I - Hotevilla

(E) Rolls not prepared in strict conformity with the above instructions will be returned for correction.

*NOTE: These instructions are directed at the Navajo census ONLY.

**NOTE: These instructions are directed at the Hopi census ONLY

CENSUS

of the

NAVAJO TRIBE Hopi

Indian Reservation of

the

Hopi Indian Agency

Arizona Jurisdiction

NAVAJO INDIAN CENSUS, (As of April 1, 1932)

KEY: Census Number; Name; Sex; Age at Last Birthday; Tribe (Navajo, unless otherwise stated); Degree of Blood; Marital Status; Relationship to Head of Family; At Jurisdiction where enrolled [Yes or No] (If no, Where); Ward [Yes or No]; Allotment, Annuity, and Identification Numbers.

1; Ace N. Terherte; m; 33 (1899); F; m; Head; yes; yes; 5649
2; Hosh Con Bitsi; f; 38 (1894); F; m; wife; yes; yes; 5724
3; Mose N. Terperte; m; 16 (1916); F; s; son; yes; yes; 5650
4; Zah Six; f; 12 (1920); F; s; dau; yes; yes; 5651
5; Sie Ye; m; 7 (1925); F; s; son; yes; yes; 5652
6; Yah She; m; 6 (1925); F; s; son; yes; yes; 5725
7; Tolie; m; 4 (1928); F; s; son; yes; yes; 5726
8; Hosh Con Bitsi #2; f; 26 (1906); F; m; wife; yes; yes; 5653
9; Nez; m; 8 (1924); F; s; son; yes; yes; 5654
10; Yazza; m; 6 (1926); F; s; son; yes; yes; 5655
11; Ah Ade Soi; f; 4 (1928); F; s; dau; yes; yes; 5656

12; Aching Leg; m; 83 (1849); F; m; Head; yes; yes; 4400
13; Bah; f; 34 (1898); F; m; wife; yes; yes; 554;
14; Charley; m; 17 (1915); F; s; son; yes; yes; 3322
15; Ah Tade Socie; f; 13 (1919); F; s; dau; yes; yes; 555
16; Nee The Bah; f; 11 (1921); F; s; dau; yes; yes; 556
17; Jah Te; m; 11 (1921); F; s; son; yes; yes; 3320
18; Dah Ad Zin; m; 9 (1923); F; s; grnd-son; yes; yes; 552

19; Ah, Aszan; f; 68 (1864); F; w; Head; yes; yes; 3997
20; Ne The He Wood; m; 2 (1930); F; s; son; yes; yes; 6060

21; Ah Ade; f; 88 (1844); F; w; Head; yes; yes; 268
22; John Nez Clanny Bitsi; f; 34 (1898); F; w; grnd-dau; yes; yes; 269
23; Ah Ade Bahhe; f; 17 (1915); F; s; grt-grnd-dau; yes; yes; 282;
24; Hoskie Ya Ne Ya; m; 13 (1919); F; s; grt-grnd-son; yes; yes; 298

25; Hoskie Na Ya; m; 12 (1920); F; s; grt-grnd-son; yes; yes; 1120
26; Hoskie ye Da Ni Ya; m; 7 (1925); F; s; grt-grnd-son; yes; yes; 270
27; Yazzie, John; f; 2 (1930); F; s son; yes; yes; 1652

28; Ah A She, Hosteen; m; ?; F; m; Head; yes; yes; 993
29; Ah A She, Hosteen, Wife; f; ?; F; m; wife; yes; yes; 974
30; Bah Yazze; f; 9 (1923); F; S; grnd-dau; yes; yes; 532

31; Ah A She Bitse, Hosteen; f; 40 (1892); F; w; Head; yes; yes; 529
32; Ah Si He; f; 17 (1915); F; s; dau; yes; yes; 3432
33; Salt, Evan; m; 11 (1921); F; s; son; yes; yes; 3433
34; Bah NE Bah; f; 5 (1927); F; s; dau; yes; yes; 533
35; Can; f; 3 (1929); F; s; dau; yes; yes; 3431

36; Ah Can Li; m; 35 (1897); F; m; Head; yes; yes; 940
37; Ah Can Li's Wife; f; 31 (1901); F; m; wife; yes; yes; 438

NAVAJO INDIAN CENSUS, (As of April 1, 1932)

KEY: Census Number; Name; Sex; Age at Last Birthday; Tribe (Navajo, unless otherwise stated); Degree of Blood; Marital Status; Relationship to Head of Family; At Jurisdiction where enrolled [Yes or No] (If no, Where); Ward [Yes or No]; Allotment, Annuity, and Identification Numbers.

38; Gucy, Robert; m; 12 (1920); F; s; son; yes; yes; 942
39; Cay Na Yah; m; 11 (1921); F; s; son; yes; yes; *(Blank)*
40; Chee; m; 9 (1923); F; s; son; yes; yes; 439
41; Yah Yuh; m; 5 (1927); F; s; son; yes; yes; 440
42; Thani; m; 3 (1929); F; s; son; yes; yes; 3478

43; Ah Chole He Cripped, Aszan; f; ?; F; w; Head; yes; yes; 115
44; Hosteen Na Ha Ah; m; 23 (1909); F; s; son; yes; yes; *(Blank)*
45; Kee On Nez; m; 22 (1910); F; s; son; yes; yes; *(Blank)*

46; Ah Cane Lee; m; 35 (1897); F; w; Head; yes; yes; 3976
47; Harold; m; 18 (1914); F; s; son; yes; yes; 3978

48; She Cay Yazze; m; 11 (1921); F; s; son; yes; yes; 4438
49; Bah Dah De; f; 9 (1923); F; s; dau; yes; yes; 3081
50; Ah She De Bah; f; 5 (1927); F; s; dau; yes; yes; 4437
51; Ha Wood Hoskie; m; 5 (1927); F; s; son; yes; yes; 3982
52; Dennit Chee; m; 4 (1928); f; s; son; yes; yes; 4105

53; Ah Chee, Aszan; f; 53 (1879); F; w; Head; yes; yes; 4107
54; Cora; f; 28 (1904); F; s; dau; yes; yes; 4436
55; Anna; f; 14 (1918); F; s; grnd-dau; yes; yes; 4439

56; Ah Chi Bitsoni; m; 38 (1894); F; m; Head; yes; yes; 4146
57; Shafgy Bema; f; 37 (1895); F; m; wife; yes; yes; 5758
58; Soi He; m; 19 (1913); F; s; son; yes; yes; 5859
59; Dah La Chee Benna; f; 26 (1906); F; s; dau; yes; yes; 5763
60; Earl; m; 16 (1916); F; s; son; yes; yes; 5757
61; Shay Chilly; m; 8 (1924); F; s; son; yes; yes; 5761
62; Na Ah Zizzie; m; 6 (1926); F; s; son; yes; yes; 5760
63; Bahhe; m; 4 (1928); F; s; son; yes; yes; 5762

64; Ah De Chi; m; 55 (1877); F; m; Head; yes; yes; *(Blank)*
65; Ah De Chi's Wife; f; 26 (1906); F; m; wife; yes; yes; 1547
66; Ye Soi; f; 9 (1925); F; s; dau; yes; yes; 1545
67; Ye Zunth; m; 7 (1925); F; s; son; yes; yes; 1549
68; Hunter, Harry; m; 4 (1928); F; s; son; yes; yes; 1548
69; Dena Soi; m; 2 (1930); F; s; son; yes; yes; 1666

70; Ah De Chi; m; ?; F; m; Head; yes; yes; 5835
71; Ah He De Bah; f; 23 (1909); F; m; wife; yes; yes; 5837
72; Big Gambler, Blanche; f; 21 (1911); F; s; dau; yes; yes; 5792
73; Ah Ade Soi, Betty Gambler; f; 4 (1928); F; s; dau; yes; yes; 5800
74; Lorenzo; m; 3 (1929); F; s; son; yes; yes; 4525

NAVAJO INDIAN CENSUS, (As of April 1, 1932)
KEY: Census Number; Name; Sex; Age at Last Birthday; Tribe (Navajo, unless otherwise stated); Degree of Blood; Marital Status; Relationship to Head of Family; At Jurisdiction where enrolled [Yes or No] (If no, Where); Ward [Yes or No]; Allotment, Annuity, and Identification Numbers.

75; Kee Soise He; m; 2 (1930); F; s; son; yes; yes; 4538

76; Ah De Chi Nez; m; 91 (1841); F; m; Head; yes; yes; 4245
77; Ah De Chi Nez's Wife; f; 31 (1901); F; m; wife; yes; yes; *(Blank)*
78; Ah Si He; f; 13 (1919); F; s; dau; yes; yes; 4342
79; Aszonie; f; 11 (1921); F; s; dau; yes; yes; *(Blank)*
80; Ah Tade Yazza; f; 9 (1923); F; s; dau; yes; yes; 4241
81; Denet Tolie; m; 5 (1927); F; s; son; yes; yes; 4240
82; Si Bahhe; m; 3 (1929); F; s; son; yes; yes; 4243

83; Ah De Chi Socie; m; ?; F; m; Head; yes; yes; 2430
84; Ah De Bay Aszan; f; 44 (1888); F; m; wife; yes; yes; 2937
85; Aszan Yazze; f; 20 (1912); F; s; dau; yes; yes; 2938
86; Nona; f; 12 (1920); F; s; dau; yes; yes; 2939
87; Ken, Ken; m; 11 (1921); F; s; son; yes; yes; 4595
88; Ken Ah Sis; f; 9 (1923); F; s; dau; yes; yes; 2940
89; Way Chilly; f; 6 (1926); F; s; dau; yes; yes; 2941
90; Ah Hosk Be Ade He; m; 4 (1928); F; s; son; yes; yes; 2431

91; Ah De Chi Socie Bedonni; m; ?; F; m; Head; yes; yes; *(Blank)*
92; Ah De Chi Socie Bedonni's Wife; f; 26 (1906); F; m; wife; yes; yes; 4231
93; Si He; f; 7 (1925); F; s; dau; yes; yes; 4232
94; Aszan Si He; f; 35 (1897); F; m; wife; yes; yes; 4233

95; Ah De Chi Socie Bay Aszan; f; 48 (1884); F; w; Head; yes; yes; 4228
96; Tah Si Ah; m; 20 (1912); F; s; son; yes; yes; *(Blank)*
97; Guy John Gold; m; 15 (1917); F; s; son; yes; yes; *(Blank)*
98; Clah; m; 13 (1919); F; s; son; yes; yes; *(Blank)*
99; Bahhe; m; 11 (1921); F; s; son; yes; yes; *(Blank)*

100; Ah De Chi Yazze; m; ?; F; m; Head; yes; yes; 3031
101; Ah De Chi Yazze Bezah Ah; f; ?; F; m; wife; yes; yes; 3034
102; Ah Ade Soi; f; 17 (1915); F; s; dau; no; Leupp School, P.O. Leupp, Coconino Co, AZ; yes; *(Blank)*
103; Ah Chee; f; 8 (1924); F; s; dau; yes; yes; 2973
104; Ah Ade Si He; f; 3 (1929); F; s; dau; yes; yes; 5314

105; Ah De Chie; m; 65 (1867); F; w; Head; yes; yes; 299

106; Ah Di Aye Yazza; m; 48 (1884); F; m; Head; yes; yes; *(Blank)*
107; Ah Di Aye Yazza Benna; f; 33 (1899); F; m; wife; yes; yes; 5663
108; Etta; f; 17 (1915); F; s; dau; yes; yes; 5664
109; Sens; m; 13 (1919); F; s; son; yes; yes; 5665
110; Sene Askisi He; m; 10 (1922); F; s; son; yes; yes; 5666

NAVAJO INDIAN CENSUS, (As of April 1, 1932)

KEY: Census Number; Name; Sex; Age at Last Birthday; Tribe (Navajo, unless otherwise stated); Degree of Blood; Marital Status; Relationship to Head of Family; At Jurisdiction where enrolled [Yes or No] (If no, Where); Ward [Yes or No]; Allotment, Annuity, and Identification Numbers.

111; Ah Ade Socie; f; 5 (1927); F; s; dau; yes; yes; 5667
112; Dah Yous; f; 23 (1909); F; w; Sis-in-law; yes; yes; 5688

113; Ah Deele, Aszan, Martin; m; ?; f; m; Head; yes; yes; *(Blank)*
114; Aszan Ah Deele's Wife; f; ?; F; m; wife; yes; yes; *(Blank)*
115; Kee Yazzie; m; 20 (1920); F; s; son; yes; yes; *(Blank)*
116; Keni; f; 18 (1914); F; s; dau; yes; yes; *(Blank)*
117; The He; m; 16 (1916); F; s; son; yes; yes; *(Blank)*
118; Keni Hez Beh; f; 14 (1918); F; s; dau; yes; yes; *(Blank)*
119; Hoski Theda; m; 12 (1920); F; s; son; yes; yes; *(Blank)*
120; Aszan Bahhe Wife #2; f; 24 (1908); F; m; wife; yes; yes; *(Blank)*
121; Red House; m; 4 (1928); F; s; son; yes; yes; *(Blank)*
122; NE Neze; m; 4 (1928); f; s; son; yes; yes; *(Blank)*

123; Ah Deeley, Aszan; f; 76 (1856); F; w; Head; yes; yes; 2482

124; Ah Ho En Tille; m; 59 (1873); F; m; Head; yes; yes; 4305
125; Aszan Toe Honani; f; 61 (1871); F; m; wife; yes; yes; 490
126; Dale; m; 30 (1902); F; s; son; yes; yes; 508
127; Bah; f; 23 (1909); F; s; dau; yes; yes; 491
128; Benny; m; 23 (1909); F; s; son; yes; yes; 498
129; Kin Yazze; m; 8 (1924); F; s; son; yes; yes; 492
130; Soi E; m; 7 (1925); F; s; son; yes; yes; 493
131; Kee Bahhe; m; 5 (1927); F; s; grnd-son; yes; yes; 494

132; Ah Hosteen; m; 53 (1879); F; m; Head; yes; yes; 1576
133; Aszan Socie; f; 43 (1889); F; m; wife; yes; yes; 1577
134; Arlie; m; 25 (1907); F; s; son; yes; yes; 1581
135; Si He; m; 16 (1916); F; s; son; yes; yes; 1582
136; Woody; m; 13 (1919); F; s; son; yes; yes; 1324
137; Kee; m; 10 (1922); F; s; son; yes; yes; 1579
138; Bah NE; m; 7 (1925); F; s; son; yes; yes; 1580

139; Ash He; f; 52 (1880); F; w; Head; yes; yes; 6457
140; Yazza; m; 35 (1897); F; s; son; yes; yes; *(Blank)*
141; Billy Wild Bill; m; 32 (1900); F; s; son; yes; yes; 6458

142; Ah See See's daughter; f; 29 (1903); F; s; dau; yes; yes; 6456
143; Esquela Bega #7; m; 25 (1907); F; s; son; yes; yes; 4506
144; Ash He; f; 20 (1912); F; s; dau; yes; yes; 6452
145; Helen Small; f; 18 (1914); F; s; dau; yes; yes; 6450
146; Socie; f; 26 (1906); F; s; grnd-dau; yes; yes; 6455
147; Tolie; f; 26 (1906); F; s; grnd-dau; yes; yes;6454
148; Yellow Hair; m; 23 (1909); F; s; grnd-son; yes; yes; 6485

NAVAJO INDIAN CENSUS, (As of April 1, 1932)

KEY: Census Number; Name; Sex; Age at Last Birthday; Tribe (Navajo, unless otherwise stated); Degree of Blood; Marital Status; Relationship to Head of Family; At Jurisdiction where enrolled [Yes or No] (If no, Where); Ward [Yes or No]; Allotment, Annuity, and Identification Numbers.

149; Frank Small; m; 21 (1911); F; s; nephew; yes; yes; 6449
150; Chee Chee; m; 15 (1917); F; s; nephew; yes; yes; 6453

151; Ahtaye, Hosteen; m; 61 (1871); F; m; Head; yes; yes; 3612
152; Zahn Guy; f; 31 (1901); F; m; wife; yes; yes; 3613
153; Deel Hoskie; m; 5 (1927); F; s; son; yes; yes; 3614

154; Ah She Badoni #1; m; 32 (1900); F; s; Head; yes; yes; 6334

155; Ah She He; m; 47 (1885); F; m; Head; yes; yes; *(Blank)*
156; Aszan Tot Soi NE; f; 46 (1886); F; m; wife; yes; yes; 170
157; Bah; f; 21 (1911); F; s; dau; yes; yes; 171
158; Yazze; m; 16 (1916); F; s; son; yes; yes; 427
159; Herman; m; 14 (1918); F; s; son; yes; yes; 911
160; Chilly; m; 12 (1920); F; s; son; yes; yes; *(Blank)*
161; Ah Tad Holani; f; 9 (1923); F; s; dau; yes; yes; 172
162; Zani Se He; f; 6 (1926); F; s; dau; yes; yes; 173

163; Ah She He; m; ?; F; m; Head; yes; yes; 3472
164; Ah She He's Wife; f; 31 (1901); F; m; wife; yes; yes; 3473
165; Kee Soi; m; 4 (1928); F; s; son; yes; yes; 3474
166; Lawrence; m; 19 (1913); F; s; nephew; yes; yes; 995

167; Ah She He Bega; m; 25 (1907); F; m; Head; yes; yes; 166
168; Bah; f; 25 (1907); F; m; wife; yes; yes; 167
169; Zani; f; 8 (1924); F; s; dau; yes; yes; 168
170; Hoskie Ne Ha Wood; m; 5 (1927); F; s; son; yes; yes; 169

171; Ah Shene Bega; m; 28 (1904); F; m; Head; yes; yes; 6475
172; Ah Shene Bega's Wife #1; 36 (1896); F; m; wife; yes; yes; 6456
173; Ah Shene Bega's Wife #2; 19 (1913); F; m; wife; yes; yes; 6482
174; Way Chonz; m; 6 (1926); F; s; son; yes; yes; 6483
175; Nah Chee; f; 4 (1928); F; s; dau; yes; yes; 6484
176; Na Glen; f; 3 (1929); F; s; dau; yes; yes; 4505
177; Hoskie Sile; m; 2 (1930); F; s; son; yes; yes; 4506

178; Ahs She, Aszan; m; 61 (1871); F; w; Head; yes; yes; 458
179; Ah She He Socie; m; 31 (1901); F; s; son; yes; yes; 928
180; Aha De Ah She He; f; 20 (1912); F; s; dau; yes; yes; 459
181; Ah Tade Na Sarde; f; 20 (1912); F; s; dau; yes; yes; 4308

182; Ahs Tale, Hosteen, Aszan; f; ?; F; w; Head; yes; yes; *(Blank)*

NAVAJO INDIAN CENSUS, (As of April 1, 1932)

KEY: Census Number; Name; Sex; Age at Last Birthday; Tribe (Navajo, unless otherwise stated); Degree of Blood; Marital Status; Relationship to Head of Family; At Jurisdiction where enrolled [Yes or No] (If no, Where); Ward [Yes or No]; Allotment, Annuity, and Identification Numbers.

183; Ahs Tale Bega, Hosteen; m; 55 (1877); F; m; Head; yes; yes; 3314
184; Ah De Chi Nez Bitse; f; 23 (1909); F; m; wife; yes; yes; 481
185; Denna Bahhe; m; 4 (1928); F; s; son; yes; yes; 3315
186; Chee; m; 10 (1922); F; s; bro-in-law; yes; yes; 478

187; Ahs Tale Bitsoni, Hosteen; m; 25 (1907); F; m; Head; yes; yes; 507
188; Ahs Na Gees Bah; f; 20 (1912); F; m; wife; yes; yes; 495
189; Aszan Chee Yazze; f; 5 (1927); F; s; dau; yes; yes; 496
190; Kee Socie Brown, Paul; m; 5 (1927); F; s; son; yes; yes; 497

191; Ah Yo Nezzie, Aszan; m; 44 (1888); F; w; Head; yes; yes; 3012
192; Asl He, Joe; m; 29 (1903); F; s; son; yes; yes; 3023
193; Kishony, Lee; m; 28 (1904); F; s; son; yes; yes; 3013
194; Kee; m; 13 (1919); F; s; son; yes; yes; 3014

195; Acade Chene; m; 46 (1886); F; m; Head; yes; yes; 3041
196; Dis Bah; f; 27 (1905); F; m; wife; yes; yes; 2822
197; Zannie Yazza; f; 11 (1921); F; s; dau; yes; yes; 2823
198; Hoskie Bahhe; m; 3 (1929); F; s; son; yes; yes; 2826
199; Aszan Bahhe; f; 15 (1917); F; s; dau; yes; yes; 2827
200; Hoskie Zohnne; m; 9 (1923); F; s; son; yes; yes; 2825

201; Apache, m; 64 (1868); F; w; Head; yes; yes; 3533
202; Socie; m; 15 (1917); F; s; son; yes; yes; 3532
203; Apache, Sylvia; f; 13 (1919); F; s; dau; yes; yes; 3534
204; Ah De; f; 15 (1927); F; s; grnd-dau; yes; yes; *(Blank)*
205; Apache; m; 13 (1913); F; s; grnd-son; yes; yes; *(Blank)*
206; Be La Ah Goody; m; 61 (1871); F; s; bro; yes; yes; 3635

207; Asche Bay; m; 40 (1892); F; w; Head; yes; yes; *(Blank)*
208; Hoskie Yath Ha Da; m; 12 (1920); F; s; son; yes; yes; 6076
209; Aszan Whoola; f; 8 (1924); F; s; dau; yes; yes; 5645
210; Si Bah Ah Goodie Yazza; m; 4 (1928); F; s; son; yes; yes; 5846
211; Aszan Cispe; f; 3 (1929); F; s; dau; yes; yes; 6074

212; Asche He; m; ?; F; w; Head; yes; yes; *(Blank)*
213; Bahhe Ad Ade; f; 22 (1910); F; s; dau; yes; yes; 3038
214; Son Sguy Zahn Kay; f; 4 (1928); F; s; grnd-dau; yes; yes; 4450

215; Aschee's Wife #2; f; 46 (1886); F; w; Head; yes; yes; 6431
216; Hosk Aschee; m; 4 (1928); F; s; son; yes; yes; 4478

217; Ashe Badoni #2; m; 24 (1907); F; w; Head; yes; yes; *(Blank)*
218; Clah; m; 20 (1912); F; s; son; yes; yes; *(Blank)*

NAVAJO INDIAN CENSUS, (As of April 1, 1932)
KEY: Census Number; Name; Sex; Age at Last Birthday; Tribe (Navajo, unless otherwise stated); Degree of Blood; Marital Status; Relationship to Head of Family; At Jurisdiction where enrolled [Yes or No] (If no, Where); Ward [Yes or No]; Allotment, Annuity, and Identification Numbers.

219; Glenn; f; 17 (1915); F; s; dau; yes; yes; *(Blank)*
220; Nez, Howard; m; 14 (1918); F; s; son; yes; yes; *(Blank)*

221; Ashe He, Aszan; m; 41 (1891); F; m; Head; yes; yes; 4307
222; Zahns Bahhe; f; 45 (1887); F; m; wife; yes; yes; *(Blank)*

223; Ashe She He; m; 33 (1899); F; m; Head; yes; yes; 2882
224; Ashe She He Bay Aszan; f; ?; F; m; wife; yes; yes; 2883
225; Chee; m; 5 (1927); F; s; son; yes; yes; 2884
226; Ah Ade; f; 4 (1928); F; s; dau; yes; yes; 2885
227; Zahn Socie; f; 18 (1914); F; s; dau; yes; yes; 2409
228; Zoe; f; 16 (1916); F; s; dau; yes; yes; 2411
229; Juanita; f; 17 (1915); F; s; dau; yes; yes; 2410
230; Sylva; f; 11 (1921); F; s; dau; yes; yes; 2412
231; Kee; m; 16 (1916); F; s; son; yes; yes; 2413
232; Hoskie Si Si; m; 28 (1904); F; s; nephew; yes; yes; *(Blank)*

233; Ash She He Socie; m; 31 (1901); F; m; Head; yes; yes; 3015
234; Hily; f; 32 (1900); F; m; wife; yes; yes; 3016
235; Zannie Yazza; f; 11 (1921); F; s; dau; yes; yes; 3017
236; Gyye; m; 9 (1923); F; s; son; yes; yes; 3352
237; Way Ah Socie; f; 7 (1925); F; s; dau; yes; yes; 3353
238; Hoskie NE She Ye; m; 5 (1927); F; s; son; yes; yes; 3018
239; Ruth; f; 3 (1929); F; s; dau; yes; yes; 3019
240; King; m; 2 (1930); F; s; son; yes; yes; 3354
241; Billy; m; 18 (1914); F; s; bro; yes; yes; 3026
242; Dena Si He; m; 21 (1911); F; s; bro; yes; yes; 3342

243; Asjans Tou; f; 68 (1964); F; w; Head; yes; yes; 3793

244; Astzan, Dale; m; 72 (1860); F; w; Head; yes; yes; 1560

245; Aye Ah Bah; m; 30 (1902); F; w; Head; yes; yes; 123
246; She Chilli, Billy Mike; m; 9 (1923); F; s; yes; yes; 29
247; Ta Ne Yah; m; 7 (1925); F; s; son; yes; yes; 118
248; Guy; m; 5 (1927); F; s; son; yes; yes; 122

249; As Zan Clock Begay; m; 42 (1890); F; m; Head; yes; yes; *(Blank)*
250; Aszan Clock Begay Ah; f; 51 (1881); F; m; wife; yes; yes; 3771
251; Kee; f; 16 (1916); F; s; dau; yes; yes; 3782
252; Bah; f; 13 (1919); F; s; dau; yes; yes; 3772
253; Yazzie Kee; m; 8 (1924); F; s; son; yes; yes; *(Blank)*

NAVAJO INDIAN CENSUS, (As of April 1, 1932)

KEY: Census Number; Name; Sex; Age at Last Birthday; Tribe (Navajo, unless otherwise stated); Degree of Blood; Marital Status; Relationship to Head of Family; At Jurisdiction where enrolled [Yes or No] (If no, Where); Ward [Yes or No]; Allotment, Annuity, and Identification Numbers.

254; B. Sam; m; 38 (1894); F; w; Head; yes; yes; *(Blank)*
255; Aszan To Ad Lena; f; 6 (1926); F; s; dau; yes; yes; 540
256; Jack; m; 5 (1927); F; s; son; yes; yes; 537
257; Betty; f; 12 (1920); F; s; Niece; yes; yes; 538

258; Badoni, Jim; m; 33 (1899); F; m; Head; yes; yes; 290
259; Bitsi; f; 25 (1907); F; m; wife; yes; yes; 266
260; Das Wood; m; 11 (1921); F; m; son; yes; yes; 278
261; Ahs Has Bah; f; 9 (1923); F; s; dau; yes; yes; 280
262; Ya; m; 6 (1926); F; s; son; yes; yes; 279
263; Bah Yazze; f; 4 (1928); F; s; dau; yes; yes; 267

264; Badoni Begay; m; 43 (1889); F; m; Head; yes; yes; 881
265; Hosteen Chee Bema; f; 38 (1894); F; m; wife; yes; yes; 782
266; Dena Yazze, David; m; 17 (1915); F; s; no; Leupp School, P.O. Leupp, Coconino Co, AZ; yes; *(Blank)*
267; Dorothy; f; 16 (1916); F; s; dau; yes; yes; 1392
268; Si Na Jinny; m; 13 (1919); F; s; son; yes; yes; 776
269; Phoebe; f; 15 (1917); F; s; dau; no; Leupp School, P.O. Leupp, Coconino Co, AZ; yes; 1670
270; Ah Ade Bahhe; f; 8 (1924); F; s; dau; yes; yes; 783
271; Badoni Be Nally; m; 19 (1913); F; s; nephew; yes; yes; *(Blank)*
272; Ruby; f; 38 (1894); F; m; wife #2; yes; yes; 775
273; Florence; f; 18 (1914); F; s; dau; yes; yes; 600

274; Bah, m; 46 (1886); F; m; Head; yes; yes; *(Blank)*
275; Clie Na Ne Bah; f; 38 (1894); F; m; wife; yes; yes; 770

276; Bah; m; ?; F; m; Head; yes; yes; *(Blank)*
277; Ah She De Bah; F; 33 (1899); F; m; wife; yes; yes; 1482
278; Denna Yazza; m; 11 (1921); F; s; son; yes; yes; *(Blank)*
279; Yo Des Bah; f; 9 (1923); F; s; dau; yes; yes; *(Blank)*
280; Bet Nanny Son; m; 7 (1925); F; s; son; yes; yes; 1486

281; Tah Des Bah; f; 5 (1927); F; s; son; yes; yes; 1483
282; Dah She Bah; f; 26 (1906); F; m; wife; yes; yes; 1484
283; Des Bah; f; 13 (1919); F; s; dau; yes; yes; 1485
284; Sally; f; 16 (1916); F; s; ?; yes; yes; 1604
285; Claw, Gordon; m; 30 (1902); F; s; ?; yes; yes; 907

286; Bah; f; 21 (1911); F; w; Head; yes; yes; 2830
287; Tollie; f; 3 (1929); F; s; dau; yes; yes; *(Blank)*
288; Florence; f; 17 (1915); F; s; ?; yes; yes; 2831
289; Charley, Dorothy; f; 13 (1918); F; s; sis; yes; yes; *(Blank)*

NAVAJO INDIAN CENSUS, (As of April 1, 1932)

KEY: Census Number; Name; Sex; Age at Last Birthday; Tribe (Navajo, unless otherwise stated); Degree of Blood; Marital Status; Relationship to Head of Family; At Jurisdiction where enrolled [Yes or No] (If no, Where); Ward [Yes or No]; Allotment, Annuity, and Identification Numbers.

290; Nez, Charley; m; 11 (1921); F; s; bro; yes; yes; 4565
291; Zahn Socie, Mary; f; 4 (1928); F; s; sis; yes; yes; 2832
*292; Tollie; f; 3 (1929); F; s; dau; yes; yes; 4562
   (*NOTE: Probably the same child as #287 above)

293; Bah; m; 61 (1871); F; w; Head; yes; yes; 3519

294; Bah; f; 27 (1905); F; w; Head; yes; yes; 4217
295; Aszan Socie, Betty; f; 21 (1911); F; s; sis; yes; yes; 4475
296; Aszan Chee Le; f; 20 (1912); F; s; sis; yes; yes; 4218
297; Way She He; f; 8 (1924); F; s; dau; yes; yes; 4219
298; Denna Yazza; m; 7 (1925); F; s; son; yes; yes; 4220

299; Bah; f; 78 (1854); F; w; Head; yes; yes; 5796

300; Bahhe Badoni; m; 34 (1898); F; w; Head; yes; yes; 263
301; Bay Yazzie; f; 3 (1929); F; s; dau; yes; yes; 1179

302; Bah He, Johnnie; m; 4 (1928); F; s; Head; yes; yes; 3527

303; Bah Ho Zone; m; 60 (1872); F; m; Head; yes; yes; 1349
304; Ah Has Bah; f; 44 (1888); F; m; wife; yes; yes; 1168
305; Aszan Nez; f; 28 (1904); F; s; stp-dau; yes; yes; 1169
306; Asoise De Bah; f; 16 (1916); F; s; dau; yes; yes; 1170
307; Nava; f; 12 (1920); F; s; dau; yes; yes; 1171
308; Dennie Socie; m; 10 (1922); F; s; son; yes; yes; 1172

309; Bah Ho Zonnie; m; ?; F; m; Head; yes; yes; 5832
310; Bah Ho Zonnie Bay Aszan; f; 43 (1889); F; m; wife; yes; yes; 5794
311; Hoskie Socie; m; 21 (1911); F; s; son; yes; yes; 5831
312; Na Bah; f; 23 (1909); F; s; dau; yes; yes; 5793
313; Zahn Soi; f; 28 (1904); F; m; wife; yes; yes; 5833
314; Ze Le Soi; m; 3 (1929); F; s; son; yes; yes; 5795
315; Chee Bahhe; m; 2 (1930); F; s; son; yes; yes; 6088

316; Bah Wanah; f; 77 (1855); F; w; Head; yes; yes; 3937
317; Hosteen Chee Be Beda; m; 25 (1907); F; s; son; yes; yes; 3930

318; Baish, Hosteen; m; 42 (1890); F; m; Head; yes; yes; 1495
319; Bah; f; 22 (1910); F; m; wife; yes; yes; 1496
320; Ha Na Ne Bah; f; 4 (1928); F; s; dau; yes; yes; 1497
321; Ayne Bah; f; 3 (1929); F; s; dau; yes; yes; 1653
322; Hoskie Yazzie; m; 2 (1930); F; s; son; yes; yes; 1654

NAVAJO INDIAN CENSUS, (As of April 1, 1932)

KEY: Census Number; Name; Sex; Age at Last Birthday; Tribe (Navajo, unless otherwise stated); Degree of Blood; Marital Status; Relationship to Head of Family; At Jurisdiction where enrolled [Yes or No] (If no, Where); Ward [Yes or No]; Allotment, Annuity, and Identification Numbers.

323; Barney; m; 37 (1895); F; s; Head; yes; yes; 2403

324; Bash Ne De Ne; m; ?; F; m; Head; yes; yes; *(Blank)*
325; Ah Na Des Bah; f; 43 (1889); F; m; wife; yes; yes; *(Blank)*

326; Baw, John; m; 25 (1907); F; m; Head; yes; yes; 3645
327; Mose's Wife; f; 31 (1901); F; m; wife; yes; yes; 3642

328; Bay De Lahe Bega; m; ?; F; m; Head; yes; yes; *(Blank)*
329; Ah Soi E Bah; f; 20 (1912); F; m; wife; yes; yes; 4236

330; Bay Gach Be Aye Be; m; 37 (1895); F; m; Head; yes; yes; 5683
331; Zah Ha Banna; f; 27 (1905); F; m; wife; yes; yes; 5678
332; Zah Ha; m; 11 (1921); F; s; son; yes; yes; 5675
333; Cho Li; m; 9 (1923); F s; son; yes; yes; 5676
334; Asch Lee; m; 6 (1926); F; s; son; yes; yes; 6032
335; Gee Tolli; m; 4 (1928); F; s; son; yes; yes; 6034

336; Be Aye De Chizzy Benna; f; 53 (1879); F; w; Head; yes; yes; 5673
337; Be Aye De Clizzy[sic]; m; 16 (1916); F; s; son; yes; yes; *(Blank)*
338; Kee Yazzie; m; 16 (1916); F; s; son; yes; yes; 5674

340; Becay; m; 73 (1859); F; m; Head; yes; yes; 3871
341; Becay's Wife; f; 62 (1870); F; m; wife; yes; yes; 3872
342; Zan Si Benna; f; 28 (1904); F; w; dau; yes; yes; 3873
343; Ah Toan Sui; f; 10 (1922); F; s; grnd-dau; yes; yes; 3874
344; To Li; m; 34 (1898); F; s; son; yes; yes; 3886
345; Az He; m; 15 (1917); F; s; son; yes; yes; 3875
346; Sells Peter; m; 20 (1912); F; s; nephew; yes; yes; 3876
347; Mabel; f; 18 (1914); F; s; niece; yes; yes; 3891
348; Aszan; Soi; f; 35 (1897); F; m; wife; yes; yes; 3878

349; Becay Bekis; m; 62 (1870); F; m; Head; yes; yes; 3700
350; Becay Bekis' Wife; f; 35 (1897); F; m; wife; yes; yes; 3701
351; Aszan De Tomne; f; 11 (1921); F; s; dau; yes; yes; 3702
352; Asta Tes Bah Connie; f; 4 (1928); F; s; dau; yes; yes; 3703
353; Yell Wood De; m; 3 (1929); F; s; son; yes; yes; 4120

354; Becay's Son-in-Law #1; m; 38 (1894); F; s; Head; yes; yes; 3887

355; Becay's Son-in-Law #2; m; 26 (1806); F; s; Head; yes; yes; 3888

356; Be Da Ah Thanny Bega, Hosteen; m; 42 (1890); F; m; Head; yes; yes; 5900
357; Na Chi De He Yea Aszan; f; 33 (1899); F; m; wife; yes; yes; 5906

NAVAJO INDIAN CENSUS, (As of April 1, 1932)
KEY: Census Number; Name; Sex; Age at Last Birthday; Tribe (Navajo, unless otherwise stated); Degree of Blood; Marital Status; Relationship to Head of Family; At Jurisdiction where enrolled [Yes or No] (If no, Where); Ward [Yes or No]; Allotment, Annuity, and Identification Numbers.

358; Zahn; f; 17 (1915); F; s; dau; yes; yes; 5907
359; Kee; m; 15 (1917); F; s; son; yes; yes; 4559
360; Kee Soi; m; 3 (1929); F; s; son; yes; yes; 4555

361; Beda Ba Ne Sazie; m; 53 (1879); F; m; Head; yes; yes; 2951
362; Beda Ba Ne Sazie's Wife; f; 31 (1901); F; m; wife; yes; yes; *(Blank)*
363; Dan; m; 13 (1919); F; s; son; no; Leupp, AZ, P.O. Leupp, Coconino Co, AZ; yes; *(Blank)*
364; Diana; f; 11 (1921); F; s; dau; no; Leupp School, P.O. Leupp, Coconino Co, AZ; yes; *(Blank)*
365; Sallie; f; 10 (1922); F; s; dau; no; Leupp School, P.O. Leupp, Coconino Co, AZ; yes; *(Blank)*
366; Denna She Bahhe; m; 8 (1924); F; s; son; yes; yes; *(Blank)*
367; Hoskie Yazzie; m; 4 (1928); F; s; son; yes; yes; *(Blank)*

368; Bedah Vannie Hosteen; m; 73 (1859); F; m; Head; yes; yes; *(Blank)*
369; Bahhe; f; 21 (1911); F; m; wife; yes; yes; *(Blank)*

370; Ye Wol Die; f; 7 (1925); F; s; dau; yes; yes; *(Blank)*
371; Chee He Hoskie; m; 4 (1928); F; s; son; yes; yes; *(Blank)*

372; Be Do Ne Aszan; f; 61 (1871); F; w; Head; yes; yes; 1474

373; Be Ga, Hosteen; m; ?; F; m; Head; yes; yes; 98
374; Ah Ade Socie; f; 25 (1907); F; m; wife; yes; yes; 2896
375; Na Ta Ne Bah; f; 4 (1928); F; s; dau; yes; yes; 2897
376; Denet Nemore; m; 2 (1930); F; s; son; yes; yes; *(Blank)*
377; Duna Ne Mozzie; m; 2 (1930); F; s; son; yes; yes; 6089
378; Da Da Ha Doody; m; ?; F; s; bro; yes; yes; *(Blank)*
379; Si Yah; m; 17 (1915); F; s; nephew; yes; yes; *(Blank)*

380; Begay, Johnnie; m; 31 (1901); F; m; Head; yes; yes; 336
381; Soh Gro Ve, Gilford; f; 34 (1898); F; m; wife; yes; yes; 174
382; Soh Gro Ve, Betty; f; 10 (1922); F; s; dau; yes; yes; 175
383; Scott, Slyvania; f; 8 (1924); F; s; dau; yes; yes; 176
384; Nad Ath He Has Bega; m; 5 (1927); F; s; son; yes; yes; 177

385; Begay, Tony; m; 27 (1905); F; m; Head; yes; yes; 315
386; Beka, Tony's Wife; f; 23 (1909); F; m; wife; yes; yes; 301
387; Noskie Nad A Ho; m; 7 (1925); F; s; son; yes; yes; 304
*387; Bahhe, Hosteen; m; 5 (1927); F; s; son; yes; yes; 316
388; Chus Chee; m; 4 (1928); F; s; son; yes; yes; 303

(*NOTE: Number listed twice)

NAVAJO INDIAN CENSUS, (As of April 1, 1932)
KEY: Census Number; Name; Sex; Age at Last Birthday; Tribe (Navajo, unless otherwise stated); Degree of Blood; Marital Status; Relationship to Head of Family; At Jurisdiction where enrolled [Yes or No] (If no, Where); Ward [Yes or No]; Allotment, Annuity, and Identification Numbers.

389; Bega #1, Charley; m; 45 (1887); F; m; Head; yes; yes; 499
390; Bah; f; 23 (1909); F; m; wife; yes; yes; 500
391; Kee Bah He; m; 5 (1927); F; s; son; yes; yes; 501

392; Bega #2; m; 33 (1899); F; w; Head; yes; yes; 454
393; Dena Socie; m; 5 (1927); F; s; son; yes; yes; *(Blank)*

394; Bega De Nege, Hosteen; m; 36 (1896); F; m; Head; yes; yes; 4455
395; Cora; f; 26 (1906); F; m; wife; yes; yes; 3651
396; Ke Ha Ne Bah; f; 9 (1923); F; s; dau; yes; yes; *(Blank)*
397; Yah Ne Bah; f; 7 (1925); F; s; dau; yes; yes; 3650
398; Ye Seth Hoskie; m; 5 (1927); F; s; son; yes; yes; 3649
399; Hoskie Na Thel; m; 4 (1928); F; s; son; yes; yes; 4454

400; Be Gande Ne, Hosteen; m; 54 (1878); F; m; Head; yes; yes; 3802
401; Be Gande Ne's, Hosteen, Wife; f; 52 (1880); F; m; wife; yes; yes; 3803
402; Waye Bahhe; f; 27 (1905); F; s; dau; yes; yes; 3804
*404; Zahn Eh He; f; 21 (1911); F; s; dau; yes; yes; 3805
405; Eityantso, Sarah; f; 19 (1913); F; s; dau; yes; yes; *(Blank)*
406; Kee Lay; m; 16 (1916); F; s; son; yes; yes; 3806
407; Na Nah Way; m; 11 (1921); F; s; son; yes; yes; 3807
  (*NOTE: #403 was omitted from original)

408; Beganepaz Mt. Bega; m; 28 (1904); F; m; Head; yes; yes; 6347
409; Naglen; f; 19 (1913); F; m; wife; yes; yes; 6348

410; Begay, Hosteen; m; 23 (1909); F; s; Head; yes; yes; 1325
411; Melvin; m; 17 (1915); F; s; bro; yes; yes; 1700
412; Bizante; m; 11 (1921); F; s; bro; yes; yes; 1629
413; Na Nez Bah; f; 8 (1924); F; s; sis; yes; yes; 1414
*413; Gath; m; 6 (1926); F; s; bro; yes; yes; 413
414; Zahne Bah; f; 5 (1927); F; s; sis; yes; yes; 1415
  (*NOTE: Number listed twice)

415; Begah Ah Jinny's, Hosteen, Wife; f; 53 (1879); F; w; Head; yes; yes; 1509

416; Be Gees, Hosteen; m; 66 (1866); F; m; Head; yes; yes; 748
417; Aszan Deel; f; 64 (1868); F; m; wife; yes; yes; 749
418; David; m; 19 (1913); F; s; son; yes; yes; *(Blank)*
419; Joel; f; 11 (1921); F; s; dau; yes; yes; 750

420; Be Gelly; m; 53 (1879); F; w; Head; yes; yes; 868

NAVAJO INDIAN CENSUS, (As of April 1, 1932)
KEY: Census Number; Name; Sex; Age at Last Birthday; Tribe (Navajo, unless otherwise stated); Degree of Blood; Marital Status; Relationship to Head of Family; At Jurisdiction where enrolled [Yes or No] (If no, Where); Ward [Yes or No]; Allotment, Annuity, and Identification Numbers.

421; Be Goody, John; m; 46 (1886); F; m; Head; yes; yes; *(Blank)*
422; Be Goody's Wife, John[sic]; f; 43 (1889); F; m; wife; yes; yes; 5887
423; Be Goody, David; m; 23 (1909); F; s; son; yes; yes; *(Blank)*
424; Kee Bahhe; m; 21 (1911); F; s; son; yes; yes; 5895
425; Aszan Deel; f; 20 (1912); F; s; dau; yes; yes; 5890
426; Kee Yazze, Norman; m; 19 (1914); F; s; son; yes; yes; 5889
427; Bahhe; m; 15 (1917); F; s; son; yes; yes; *(Blank)*
428; Chonne, Roger; m; 14 (1918); F; s; son; yes; yes; 5892
429; Zah Yazzie; f; 11 (1921); F; s; dau; yes; yes; 5893
430; Si Soi; m; 9 (1923); F; s; son; yes; yes; 5885
431; Hoskie Bahhe; m; 8 (1924); F; s; son; yes; yes; 5894
432; Socie; f; 6 (1926); F; s; dau; yes; yes; 5891
433; Bah; f; 4 (1928); F; s; dau; yes; yes; 5888

434; Be Goody #2, John; m; 41 (1891); F; m; Head; yes; yes; 2887
435; Begoody Aszan, John[sic]; f; 39 (1893); F; m; wife; yes; yes; 2888
436; Yazza, Annie; f; 19 (1913); F; m; wife; yes; yes; 4582

437; Bejesi Be Yaz; m; 23 (1908); F; m; Head; yes; yes; 5657
438; Hosh Con Bitsi; f; 31 (1901); F; m; wife; yes; yes; 5658
439; Ah Socie; m; 11 (1921); F; s; son; yes; yes; 5659
440; Dene Socie; m; 9 (1923); F; s; son; yes; yes; 5660
441; Aszan Bahhe; f; 7 (1925); F; s; son; yes; yes; 5661
442; Zedoso Howbiz; f; 5 (1927); F; s; dau; yes; yes; 5662
443; Yel Ne Kay; m; 4 (1928); F; s; son; yes; yes; 4540

444; Be Lee Na Ge; m; ?; F; m; Head; yes; yes; 3321
445; Be Lee Na Ge's Wife; f; 43 (1889); F; m; wife; yes; yes; 509
446; Dennis; m; 21 (1911); F; s; son; yes; yes; 510
447; Du Yah; m; 19 (1913); F; s; son; yes; yes; 514
448; Chee Kan; f; 7 (1925); F; s; dau; yes; yes; 511
449; Chee Ne Dah; f; 5 (1927); F; s; dau; yes; yes; 512
450; Chi Che Tade Bahhe; f; 18 (1914); F; s; niece; yes; yes; 513

451; Be Lin Je Zinney Benna; f; 70 (1862); F; w; Head; yes; yes; 5680
452; Tollie; m; 3 (1929); F; s; son; yes; yes; 6026
453; Chonne; f; 9 (1923); F; s; grnd-dau; yes; yes; 5682

454; Be Lon Bega; m; ?; F; m; Head; yes; yes; 1635
455; Ah Ade; f; 9 (1923); F; s; dau; yes; yes; *(Blank)*
456; Clah Bahhe; m; 6 (1926); F; s; son; yes; yes; 1475
457; Kee Soi; m; 5 (1927); F; s; son; yes; yes; 1476
458; Na Gleen Na Ne Bahhe; f; 28 (1904); F; m; wife; yes; yes; 1477
459; Socie; m; 7 (1925); F; s; son; yes; yes; 1478

NAVAJO INDIAN CENSUS, (As of April 1, 1932)

KEY: Census Number; Name; Sex; Age at Last Birthday; Tribe (Navajo, unless otherwise stated); Degree of Blood; Marital Status; Relationship to Head of Family; At Jurisdiction where enrolled [Yes or No] (If no, Where); Ward [Yes or No]; Allotment, Annuity, and Identification Numbers.

460; Ah Ade Bahhe; f; 6 (1925); F; s; dau; yes; yes; 1479
461; Ah Ade Nezzie; f; 4 (1928); F; s; dau; yes; yes; 1480
462; Denna Kai; m; 3 (1929); F; s; son; yes; yes; 1537

463; Ben, Jim; m; ?; F; m; Head; yes; yes; *(Blank)*
464; Ha Goes Bah Denna; f; 33 (1899); F; m; wife; yes; yes; 3
465; Ha Gees Bah; f; 10 (1922); F; s; dau; yes; yes; 4
466; Denet Soi; m; 8 (1924); F; s; son; yes; yes; 5
467; Bah Ne Yah; m; 4 (1928); F; s; son; yes; yes; 6

468; Ben, John; m; 31 (1901); F; w; Head; yes; yes; 390
469; Ben, James; m; 6 (1926); F; s; son; yes; yes; 392
470; Ben, Joy; f; 4 (1928); F; s; dau; yes; yes; 393

471; Bena Bahhe, Aszan; f; 57 (1875); F; w; Head; yes; yes; 2906

472; Be Na Le Bahhe, Hosteen; m; 53 (1879); F; m; Head; yes; yes; *(Blank)*
473; Aszan Sone; f; 43 (1889); F; m; wife; yes; yes; 3992
474; Si He; f; 8 (1924); F; s; niece; yes; yes; 3011

475; Be Na Te He; m; 59 (1873); F; m; Head; yes; yes; 5699
476; Be Na Te He's Wife; f; 59 (1873); F; m; wife; yes; yes; 5623
477; Akke Nez Benna; f; 43 (1889); F; w; dau; yes; yes; 5829
478; Aske Nez; m; 5 (1927); F; s; son; yes; yes; 5626
479; Ah Ade Nez; f; 4 (1928); F; s; dau; yes; yes; 5627
480; Ade Ade Sahe Benna; f; 23 (1909); F; w; dau; yes; yes; 5625

481; Benoto He Bena; m; 21 (1911); F; s; son; yes; yes; 4547
482; Kee Chee; m; 3 (1929); F; s; son; yes; yes; 4545
483; Tane Bah Yazzie; f; 2 (1930); F; s; dau; yes; yes; 4546
484; Ad Ade So He; f; 6 (1926); F; s; grnd-dau; yes; yes; 5628
485; Denna Be Yazzie; f; 5 (1927); F; s; grnd-dau; yes; yes; 5629

486; Benna, Eddie; m; ?; F; w; Head; yes; yes; 4257
487; Lettie; f; 22 (1910); F; s; dau; yes; yes; *(Blank)*
488; Aszan Nez; f; 21 (1911); F; s; dau; yes; yes; *(Blank)*
489; Sa Thli; m; 19 (1913); F; s; son; yes; yes; *(Blank)*
490; Jean; f; 15 (1917); F; s; dau; yes; yes; *(Blank)*

491; Benna, Hosteen; m; 68 (1864); F; m; Head; yes; yes; 4062
492; Benna's, Hosteen, Wife; f; 62 (1870); F; m; wife; yes; yes; 4224
493; Aszan Gle He; f; ?; F; w; mother; yes; yes; 4226
494; Away Bega; m; 11 (1921); F; s; grnd-son; yes; yes; *(Blank)*

NAVAJO INDIAN CENSUS, (As of April 1, 1932)

KEY: Census Number; Name; Sex; Age at Last Birthday; Tribe (Navajo, unless otherwise stated); Degree of Blood; Marital Status; Relationship to Head of Family; At Jurisdiction where enrolled [Yes or No] (If no, Where); Ward [Yes or No]; Allotment, Annuity, and Identification Numbers.

495; Benna, Ken; m; ?; F; w; Head; yes; yes; 5883
496; Shepherd, Donald; m; 27 (1905); F; s; son; yes; yes; 2806
497; Solzie; m; 11 (1921); F; s; grnd-son; yes; yes; 5884

498; Benny; m; 40 (1892); F; m; Head; yes; yes; 3556
499; Ta Bahhe; f; 37 (1895); F; m; wife; yes; yes; 3557
500; Ye Sone Bah; f; 14 (1918); F; s; dau; yes; yes; 3558
501; Luella; f; 32 (1900); F; s; ?; yes; yes; 3559
502; Beny Nezzie; m; 30 (1902); F; s; ?; yes; yes; 3560
503; Yazza Hoskie; m; 8 (1924); F; s; son; yes; yes; 3561
504; Bah; f; 6 (1926); F; s; dau; yes; yes; 3562
505; Has Wood; m; 4 (1928); F; s; son; yes; yes; 3563

506; Be Sa Va Clanny Bega, Hosteen; m; 38 (1894); F; m; Head; yes; yes; 1315
507; Goth Bema; f; 21 (1911); F; m; wife; yes; yes; 235
508; Soi; m; 8 (1924); F; s; son; yes; yes; 1316
509; Goth; m; 7 (1925); F; s; son; yes; yes; 262
510; Da Nas Bah; f; 5 (1927); F; s; dau; yes; yes; *(Blank)*
511; Ned; m; 24 (1908); F; s; ?; yes; yes; 237
512; Bryant; m; 29 (1903); F; s; ?; yes; yes; 1317

513; Be Sinny Badoni, Hosteen; m; 63 (1869); F; m; Head; yes; yes; 993
514; Be Sinny Hosteen, Bitse; f; 45 (1889); F; m; wife; yes; yes; *(Blank)*
515; Edgar; m; 21 (1911); F; s; son; yes; yes; *(Blank)*
516; Felix; m; 19 (1913); F; s; son; yes; yes; 994

517; Be Tone Socie; m; 43 (1889); F; m; Head; yes; yes; 1501
518; Ya Des Bah; f; 61 (1871); F; m; wife #1; yes; yes; 1503
519; Yah Nah Bah; f; 32 (1900); F; m; wife #2; yes; yes; 1504
520; Hoskie Ye Na Soi; m; 18 (1914); F; s; son; yes; yes; 1505
521; Clark, Robert; m; 19 (1913); F; s; son; yes; yes; 1644
522; Casper; m; 13 (1919); F; s; son; yes; yes; *(Blank)*
523; Katherine; f; 11 (1921); F; s; dau; yes; yes; 1643
524; Tah Na Bah; f; 9 (1923); F; s; dau; yes; yes; 1506
525; Glee Ha Bah; f; 7 (1925); F; s; dau; yes; yes; 1507
526; Hoskie Na Aye Da Yah; m; 5 (1927); F; s; son; yes; yes; 1508
527; Haske Haswood; m; 3 (1929); F; s; son; yes; yes; 1642

528; Betoni; m; 65 (1867); F; m; Head; yes; yes; 1557
529; Betoni's Wife; f; 58 (1874); F; m; wife; yes; yes; 1558
530; Badoni Bitsi; f; 36 (1896); F; w; dau; yes; yes; 1561
531; Bah; f; 10 (1922); F; s; Grnd-dau; yes; yes; 1562
532; Guy He; m; 7 (1925); F; s; grnd-son; yes; yes; 1563

NAVAJO INDIAN CENSUS, (As of April 1, 1932)
KEY: Census Number; Name; Sex; Age at Last Birthday; Tribe (Navajo, unless otherwise stated); Degree of Blood; Marital Status; Relationship to Head of Family; At Jurisdiction where enrolled [Yes or No] (If no, Where); Ward [Yes or No]; Allotment, Annuity, and Identification Numbers.

533; Hosteen Gene; m; 83 (1849); F; w; Uncle; yes; yes; *(Blank)*

534; Be Zhan Ne Dally, Hosteen; m; 61 (1871); F; w; Head; yes; yes; 2810

535; Be Ya Ye, Hosteen; m; 82 (1850); F; m; Head; yes; yes; 1573

536; Be Yelle Becla; m; 51 (1881); F; w; Head; yes; yes; 3974
537; Zannie Bahhe; f; 33 (1899); F; w; dau; yes; yes; 3091
538; Shay Way; m; 11 (1921); F; s; grnd-son; yes; yes; 3092
539; Be Yelle; m; 53 (1879); F; w; bro; yes; yes; 3810

540; Be Yo Chee Do; m; 60 (1872); F; m; Head; yes; yes; 3785
541; Aszan Nez; f; 61 (1871); F; m; wife; yes; yes; 3728
542; Ak Ad So Bega; m; 41 (1891); F; w; son; yes; yes; 3729
543; Nic Ge Ha Talye Bitse; f; 33 (1899); F; w; dau; yes; yes; 3730
544; Aszan Socie; f; 19 (1913); F; s; grnd-dau; yes; yes; 3731

545; Beza Da Bega; m; 28 (1904); F; m; Head; yes; yes; 5777
546; De Sho; f; 25 (1907); F; m; wife; yes; yes; 6099

547; Be Za De; m; 24 (1908); F; w; Head; yes; yes; 6500
548; Ah Ade; f; 8 (1924); F; s; dau; yes; yes; 5695
549; Cesoar Selago; m; ?; F; s; son; yes; yes; 5698

550; Bena The Be; f; ?; F; s; dau; yes; yes; 5699
551; Be Za De; m; ?; F; s; son; yes; yes; 6501

552; Beza De Bay Aszan; m; 58 (1874); F; w; Head; yes; yes; 6080
553; Etsidy; m; 19 (1913); F; s; grnd-son; yes; yes; *(Blank)*

554; Bezan De Nec Bega, Hosteen; m; 38 (1904); F; s; Head; yes; yes; *(Blank)*

555; Be Zit Ben; m; 49 (1883); F; m; Head; yes; yes; 4443
556; Aszan Yezzie; f; 50 (1882); F; m; wife; yes; yes; 4444
557; Zah Sice He; f; 11 (1921); F; s; dau; yes; yes; 4474

558; Bidony Sonny; m; 73 (1859); F; w; Head; yes; yes; 5207

559; Big Jim; m; 60 (1872); F; m; Head; yes; yes; 159
560; Big Jim's Wife; f; 53 (1879); F; m; wife; yes; yes; 160
561; Kee; m; 17 (1915); F; s; son; yes; yes; 918
562; Socie; m; 25 (1907); F; s; nephew; yes; yes; 919

NAVAJO INDIAN CENSUS, (As of April 1, 1932)

KEY: Census Number; Name; Sex; Age at Last Birthday; Tribe (Navajo, unless otherwise stated); Degree of Blood; Marital Status; Relationship to Head of Family; At Jurisdiction where enrolled [Yes or No] (If no, Where); Ward [Yes or No]; Allotment, Annuity, and Identification Numbers.

563; Big John; m; 49 (1883); F; m; Head; yes; yes; 140
564; Big John's Wife; f; 48 (1884); F; m; wife; yes; yes; 146
565; Dis Goody; m; 10 (1922); F; s; son; yes; yes; 113
566; Dis Bah, Mary Brown; f; 4 1928); F; s; dau; yes; yes; 129

567; Big Man; m; 29 (1903); F; m; Head; yes; yes; 1420
568; Kee Ony Nez Be Nally; f; 23 (1909); F; m; wife; yes; yes; 1421
569; Otho N. Poole; m; 18 (1914); F; s; son; yes; yes; 1422
570; Ruby; f; 17 (1915); F; s; dau; yes; yes; *(Blank)*
571; Harry; m; 14 (1918); F; s; son; yes; yes; 1618

572; Priscilla; f; 12 (1920); F; s; dau; yes; yes; *(Blank)*

573; Big Pete; m; 61 (1871); F; m; Head; yes; yes; 147
574; Aszan Ah Si He; f; 61 (1871); F; m; wife; yes; yes; 131
575; Ne Azhs; f; 16 (1916); F; s; grnd-dau; yes; yes; 117
576; Ah Bay; Wilson Archie; m; 16 (1916); F; s; nephew; yes; yes; 17

577; Billy; m; ?; F; m; Head; yes; yes; 573
578; Bah; f; 21 (1911); F; m; wife; yes; yes; 288
579; Yade Dah; f; 6 (1926); F; s; dau; yes; yes; 290
580; Nad Ads Nad As; m; 8 (1924); F; s; orphan; yes; yes; 289
581; Ta Bah Ha Socie; m; 20 (1912); F; s; ?; yes; yes; 575

582; Billy, John; m; 36 (1896); F; m; Head; yes; yes; 1365
583; Ah Ade Soi Bema; f; 26 (1906); F; m; wife; yes; yes; 831
584; Ah Ade Soi; f; 8 (1924); F; s; dau; yes; yes; 1364
585; Zani Yazze; f; 6 (1926); F; s; dau; yes; yes; 833
586; Hoskie Yo Ga; m; 5 (1927); F; s; son; yes; yes; 834
587; Billy, Mary; f; 2 (1930); F; s; dau; yes; yes; 1366

588; Billy, Jim; m; 25 (1907); F; m; Head; yes; yes; 359
589; Billy Catherine; f; 23 (1909); F; m; wife; yes; yes; 360
590; Billy, Katy; f; 4 (1928); F; s; dau; yes; yes; 361
591; Lavo, John; m; 2 (1930); F; s; son; yes; yes; 959
592; Ah Aye Yazze; f; 5 (1927); F; s; dau; yes; yes; 357

593; Billy Pete, Old; m; 65 (1867); F; m; Head; yes; yes; 908
594; Bah Yeth Ne; f; 65 (1867); F; m; wife; yes; yes; 855
595; Na Gle Ha Bah; f; 83 (1849); F; w; mother; yes; yes; 856
596; Gle Ha Bah; f; 43 (1889); F; m; wife #2; yes; yes; 863
597; He De Cho Le; m; 32 (1900); F; w; son; yes; yes; 1377
598; Yazze, Billy; m; 22 (1910); F; s; son; yes; yes; *(Blank)*

NAVAJO INDIAN CENSUS, (As of April 1, 1932)
KEY: Census Number; Name; Sex; Age at Last Birthday; Tribe (Navajo, unless otherwise stated); Degree of Blood; Marital Status; Relationship to Head of Family; At Jurisdiction where enrolled [Yes or No] (If no, Where); Ward [Yes or No]; Allotment, Annuity, and Identification Numbers.

599; Bish Be Toe Badone; m; ?; F; m; Head; yes; yes; 1383
600; Tas Dah; f; 38 (1894); F; m; wife; yes; yes; 857

601; Bitiny Goy Hostine; m; 65 (1867); F; m; Head; yes; yes; 6316
602; Keeho Benna; f; 43 (1889); F; m; wife; yes; yes; 6317
603; Wana Wood Hoskie; m; 29 (19030); F; s; son; yes; yes; 6318
604; Dashene, Lottie; f; 26 (1906); F; s; dau; yes; yes; 6319
605; Botsio Gpu Bega; m; 24 (1908); F; s; son; yes; yes; 6320
606; Ye Bah De Wood Hoskie; m; 20 (1912); F; s; son; yes; yes; 6321
607; Ta Des Wood; m; 18 (1914); F; s; son; yes; yes; 6322
608; Yazza Hoskie; m; 16 (1916); F; s; son; yes; yes; 6323
609; Chee; f; 9 (1923); F; s; dau; yes; yes; 6324
610; Yinasban; m; 5 (1927); F; s; grnd-son; yes; yes; 6325
611; Hitulia Deyanawood; f; 28 (1904); F; m; wife; yes; yes; *(Blank)*
612; Sa Nenah; f; 9 (1923); F; s; dau; yes; yes; 6326
613; Ash Cuy, White Girl; f; 6 (1926); F; s; dau; yes; yes; 6327
614; Aha Yazza; f; 4 (1928); F; s; dau; yes; yes; 6328

615; Bit An Ne Aszan #2; f; 63 (1869); F; w; Head; yes; yes; 1487

616; Bitse Bahhe, Hosteen; m; 77 (1855); F; w; Head; yes; yes; 2924

617; Bitsey Becay's Daughter; f; ?; F; w; Head; yes; yes; 3864
618; See He; f; 12 (1920); F; s; dau; yes; yes; 3870
619; Tolea; m; 10 (1922); F; s; son; yes; yes; *(Blank)*
620; Zanni; f; 6 (1926); F; s; dau; yes; yes; 3868
621; Sah Bah He; f; 7 (1925); F; s; dau; yes; yes; 3865
622; Zi Si Si; m; 5 (1927); F; s; son; yes; yes; 3867
623; Jane; f; 3 (1929); F; s; dau; yes; yes; 4467

624; Bitsi Goody; m; 43 (1889); F; m; Head; yes; yes; 866
625; To Dis Dah Dena; f; 36 (1896); F; m; wife; yes; yes; 669
626; Na Glic Ah Lee De Dah; f; 11 (1921); F; s; dau; yes; yes; 870
627; Ta Dis Bah, Vera; f; 15 (1917); F; s; dau; yes; yes; *(Blank)*
628; Ah He Ne Bah; f; 6 (1926); F; s; dau; yes; yes; 871

629; Bitsie Le Bahhe, Aszan; f; 76 (1856); F; w; Head; yes; yes; 2468

630; Bitsie Le Bahhe Bega, Hosteen; m; 34 (1898); F; m; Head; yes; yes; 2453
631; Bitsie Le Bahhe Bega's, Hosteen Wife; f; 32 (1900); F; m; wife; yes; yes; 2454
632; Kee Bahhe; m; 5 (1927); F; s; son; yes; yes; 2455

633; Bitsoni Hosteen An Asis; m; 22 (1910); F; m; Head; yes; yes; 3017
634; Aszan Se He; f; 22 (1910); F; m; wife; yes; yes; 3018

NAVAJO INDIAN CENSUS, (As of April 1, 1932)
KEY: Census Number; Name; Sex; Age at Last Birthday; Tribe (Navajo, unless otherwise stated); Degree of Blood; Marital Status; Relationship to Head of Family; At Jurisdiction where enrolled [Yes or No] (If no, Where); Ward [Yes or No]; Allotment, Annuity, and Identification Numbers.

635; Bitsoni Yellow Horse; m; 48 (1884); F; m; Head; yes; yes; 3601
636; Zannie Benna; f; 33 (1899); F; m; wife; yes; yes; 3605
637; Zannie; f; 18 (1914); F; s; dau; yes; yes; 3626
638; Chee Dena Begay; m; 26 (1906); F; s; ?; yes; yes; *(Blank)*

639; Bitsy Bitsoci Badoni; m; 47 (1885); F; m; Head; yes; yes; 2839
640; Bitsy Bitsoci's Wife; f; 25 (1907); F; m; wife; yes; yes; 2833
641; Yellow Hair, Chester; m; 19 (1913); F; s; son; yes; yes; 4599
642; Dena Socie, Ross; m; 17 (1915); F; s; son; yes; yes; 2834
643; Roy; m; 14 (1918); F; s; son; yes; yes; 2835
644; Hoskie Yazza; m; 11 (1921); F; s; son; yes; yes; 4600
645; Mark; m; 9 (1923); F; s; son; yes; yes; 2837
646; Elizabeth; f; 4 (1928); F; s; dau; yes; yes; 2836
647; Des Bah; f; 6 (1926); F; s; dau; yes; yes; 2838
648; Hosteen Socie Yazzie; m; 2 (1930); F; s; son; yes; yes; 4697

649; Bitsy Bitsoni Sonne; m; 57 (1875); F; m; Head; yes; yes; 3629
650; Bah Bena Yellow Hair's Wife; f; 57 (1875); F; m; wife; yes; yes; 3628
651; Yellow Hair, Esther; f; 16 (1916); F; s; dau; yes; yes; 3630

652; Bizah Haloni; m; 42 (1890); F; w; Head; yes; yes; 3668
653; Do So He; f; 17 (1915); F; s; dau; yes; yes; 3782
654; Ray; m; 16 (1916); F; s; son; yes; yes; 3680
655; Elmer; m; 14 (1918); F; s; son; yes; yes; 3681
656; Way Soi; m; 3 (1929); F; s; son; yes; yes; 4496
657; Aszaynnie; f; 18 (1914); F; s; niece; yes; yes; 3670
658; Bah Na Gus; f; 32 (1900); F; s; ?; yes; yes; 3671

659; Bizah Haloni, Hosteen; m; 60 (1872); F; w; Head; yes; yes; 2983

660; Black Horse; m; 38 (1894); F; w; Head; yes; yes; 5824
661; Yazza Black Horse; f; 21 (1911); F; s; dau; yes; yes; 5825

662; Black Man's Son; m; 40 (1892); F; m; Head; yes; yes; 477
663; Ken Yazz's Mother; f; 30 (1902); F; m; wife; yes; yes; 184
664; He Dog Wood; m; 8 (1924); F; s; son; yes; yes; 935
665; Hon Yazze; f; 6 (1926); F; s; dau; yes; yes; 185
666; Ah Tade; f; 4 (1928); F; s; dau; yes; yes; 186
667; Socie, Charley; m; 24 (1908); F; s; ?; yes; yes; *(Blank)*
668; Na Ma Zec; f; 19 (1913); F; s; ?; yes; yes; 931
669; Billy; m; 2 (1930); F; s; son; yes; yes; 937

NAVAJO INDIAN CENSUS, (As of April 1, 1932)
KEY: Census Number; Name; Sex; Age at Last Birthday; Tribe (Navajo, unless otherwise stated); Degree of Blood; Marital Status; Relationship to Head of Family; At Jurisdiction where enrolled [Yes or No] (If no, Where); Ward [Yes or No]; Allotment, Annuity, and Identification Numbers.

670; Black Mustache; m; 35 (1897); F; m; Head; yes; yes; 3915
671; Black Mustache's Wife; f; 31 (1901); F; m; wife; yes; yes; 3952
672; Na Ah Zizzy; m; 58 (1874); F; w; father; yes; yes; 3953
673; Ad De Chonnie; m; 7 (1925); F; s; son; yes; yes; 3954
674; Zahn Nezzie; f; 4 (1928); F; s; dau; yes; yes; 6069
675; Nezzie Hoskie, Dan; m; 18 (1914); F; s; bro-in-law; yes; yes; *(Blank)*

676; Black Sheep, Woody; m; 27 (1905); F; m; Head; yes; yes; 67
677; Black Sheep, Annie; f; 24 (1908); F; m; wife; yes; yes; 69

678; Black Sheep's Wife; f; ?; F; w; Head; yes; yes; *(Blank)*

679; Blind Woman; f; 67 (1865); F; w; Head; yes; yes; 3979

680; Blue Lake's Son; m; 24 (1908); F; s; Head; yes; yes; 3724
681; Sah Aye; m; 5 (1927); F; s; nephew; yes; yes; 3726
682; Ad Ade Se He; f; 3 (1929); F; s; niece; yes; yes; 3723
683; Stephen; m; 19 (1913); F; s; bro; yes; yes; 3722
684; Johnnie; f; 17 (1915); F; s; sis; yes; yes; 3720
685; Socie; m; 11 (1921); F; s; bro; yes; yes; 3725
686; Keh; f; 7 (1925); F; s; sis; yes; yes; 3721
687; Chlesh; f; 5 (1927); F; s; sis; yes; yes; 3719

688; Boots; m; 23 (1909); F; s; Head; yes; yes; 3998

689; Bridge, John; m; 48 (1884); F; w; Head; yes; yes; 803
690; Yazze; f; 17 (1915); F; s; dau; yes; yes; 1390
691; Ye Nez Bah; f; 12 (1920); F; s; dau; yes; yes; 805
692; Hoskie Na Yah; m; 9 (1923); F; s; son; yes; yes; 806
693; Cle Has Bah; f; 8 (1924); F; s; dau; yes; yes; 807

694; Bucking Horse's Mother; f; 85 (1847); F; w; Head; yes; yes; 551
695; Aching Leg's Daughter; f; 34 (1898); F; s; dau; yes; yes; 3324

696; Bucking Horse's Son; m; 27 (1905); F; m; Head; yes; yes; 515
697; Soe Benna; f; 29 (1903); F; m; wife; yes; yes; 3811
698; Soe; m; 7 (1925); F; s; son; yes; yes; 3812
699; Al Di De Bah; f; 2 (1930); F; s; dau; yes; yes; 4453

700; Burt; m; 25 (1907); F; m; Head; yes; yes; *(Blank)*
701; Black, Anna; f; 23 (1909); F; m; wife; yes; yes; 527
702; Caw, Jane; f; 18 (1914); F; s; sis; yes; yes; *(Blank)*
703; Hoskie Ah Si He; m; 8 (1924); F; s; bro; yes; yes; 526
704; Bina Chee; m; 10 (1922); F; s; bro; yes; yes; 524

NAVAJO INDIAN CENSUS, (As of April 1, 1932)

KEY: Census Number; Name; Sex; Age at Last Birthday; Tribe (Navajo, unless otherwise stated); Degree of Blood; Marital Status; Relationship to Head of Family; At Jurisdiction where enrolled [Yes or No] (If no, Where); Ward [Yes or No]; Allotment, Annuity, and Identification Numbers.

705; Dick; m; 23 (1909); F; s; bro; yes; yes; *(Blank)*

706; Carl; m; 24 (1908); F; m; Head; yes; yes; *(Blank)*
707; Emma; f; 20 (1912); F; m; wife; yes; yes; *(Blank)*

708; Cash Goulie; m; 76 (1856); F; m; Head; yes; yes; 6412
709; Cash Goulie's Wife; f; 68 (1864); F; m; wife; yes; yes; 4528
710; Cash Goulie's Daughter; f; ?; F; s; dau; yes; yes; 6414
711; Pat; m; 21 (1911); F; s; grnd-son; yes; yes; 6413

712; Cash Goulie Bega; m; ?; F; m; Head; yes; yes; 6491
713; Benna; f; 33 (1899); F; m; wife; yes; yes; 6407
714; Ah Aye Ke; f; 11 (1921); F; s; dau; yes; yes; 6408
715; Ah; f; 11 (1921); F; s; dau; yes; yes; 6409
716; De Nah Ah Daye; m; 7 (1925); F; s; son; yes; yes; 6410
717; Zahn Nie; f; 4 (1928); F; s; dau; yes; yes; 6411
718; Has Nez Bah; f; 3 (1929); F; s; dau; yes; yes; 4520

719; Cash Gro Lie Bega; m; 56 (1876); F; m; Head; yes; yes; 6492
720; Hosteen Blind's Daughter; f; 33 (1899); F; m; wife; yes; yes; 6493
721; Bah Ye Nie; f; 15 (1917); F; s; dau; yes; yes; 6004
722; Lorenzo; m; 11 (1921); F; s; son; yes; yes; 6494
723; Than, Willie Kay; m; 10 (1922); F; s; son; yes; yes; 6005
724; Yazza Aye; f; 8 (1924); F; s; dau; yes; yes; 6006
725; Yazza Hoskie; m; 6 (1926); F; s; son; yes; yes; 6496
726; Bah Nah; f; 4 (1928); F; s; dau; yes; yes; 6495
727; Yah Na Byanna; m; 7 (1925); F; s; son; yes; yes; *(Blank)*

728; Cash Grolie Bega #4; m; 32 (1900); F; m; Head; yes; yes; 6043
729; Cash Grolie Begay's Wife #2; f; 75 (1857); F; m; wife; yes; yes; 6042
730; Zonnie; m; 22 1910: F; s; son; yes; yes; 5738
731; Muzzie; m; 20 (1912); F; s; son; yes; yes; *(Blank)*
732; Sihe; m; 18 (1914); F; s; son; yes; yes; 6044
733; Zahne, Genevieve; f; 16 (1916); F; s; dau; no; Ft. Apache, P.O. Ft. Apache, Navajo Co, AZ; yes; 6045
734; Bahha, Hevelle; f; 14 (1918); F; s; dau; no; Ft. Apache, P.O. Ft. Apache, Navajo Co, AZ; yes; 6046
735; Jo Le La, Helen; f; 12 (1920); F; dau; no; Ft. Apache, P.O. Ft. Apache, Navajo Co, AZ; yes; 6047
736; Kee; m; 9 (1923); F; s; son; yes; yes; 6048
737; Jola; m; 7 (1925); F; s; son; yes; yes; 6049
738; Zahn; f; 3 (1929); F; s; dau; yes; yes; *(Blank)*
739; Sa Da Skezen Bay Aszan; f; 43 (1889); F; m; wife; #1; yes; yes; 5740

NAVAJO INDIAN CENSUS, (As of April 1, 1932)
KEY: Census Number; Name; Sex; Age at Last Birthday; Tribe (Navajo, unless otherwise stated); Degree of Blood; Marital Status; Relationship to Head of Family; At Jurisdiction where enrolled [Yes or No] (If no, Where); Ward [Yes or No]; Allotment, Annuity, and Identification Numbers.

740; She Cay Be Jay Bitsi; f; 34 (1898); F; w; dau; yes; yes; 5741
741; Na Ne Ne He; m; 10 (1922); F; s; grnd-son; yes; yes; 5742
742; To Bah Des Clinny, Herbert; m; 7 (1925); F; s; grnd-son; yes; yes; 6052
743; Ah De Cay; m; 8 (1924); F; s; grnd-son; yes; yes; 6053
744; Dah He; f; 6 (1926); F; s; dau; yes; yes; 6056
745; Zahn Socie; f; 6 (1926); F; s; grnd-dau; yes; yes; 6055

746; Cay Bean De; m; ?; F; m; Head; yes; yes; *(Blank)*
747; Bah Bema; f; 33 (1899); F; m; wife; yes; yes; 20
748; Bahhe, Charley; m; 16 (1916); F; s; son; yes; yes; *(Blank)*
749; Beala Gee Bah; f; 12 (1920: F; s; dau; yes; yes; 23
750; Bay Ah La; m; 11 (1921); F; s; son; yes; yes; 22
751; Li He, Jerry; m; 9 (1923); F; s; son; yes; yes; 25
752; Kee Socie; m; 6 (1926); F; s; son; yes; yes; *25 *(*NOTE: Number given twice)*
753; Peterson, Farmer; m; 10 (1922); F; s; son; yes; yes; 2947
754; Peterson, Gloria; f; 3 (1929); F; s; dau; yes; yes; 1177
755; Aszan Socie; f; 4 (1928); F; s; dau; yes; yes; 21
756; Hoskie; m; 2 (1930); F; s; son; yes; yes; 1145

757; Cha Hay Thompson, Charley; m; 53 (1879); F; m; Head; yes; yes; 201
758; Chen Has Bah, Emma; f; 28 (1904); F; m; wife; yes; yes; 202
759; Smith, Samuel; m; 9 (1925); F; s; son; yes; yes; 203
760; Stanley; m; 24 (1908); F; s; son; yes; yes; *(Blank)*
761; Ione; f; 20 (1912); F; s; dau; yes; yes; 205
762; Smith, Enoch; m; 16 (1916); F; s; son; no; Ft. Apache, P.O. Ft. Apache, Navajo Co, AZ; yes; *(Blank)*
763; Si Bahhe; m; 13 (1919); F; s; son; yes; yes; 1157

764; Cha He Bega; m; 40 (1892); F; m; Head; yes; yes; *(Blank)*
765; Bah; f; 33 (1899); F; m; wife; yes; yes; 229
766; Sam; m; 23 (1909); F; s; son; no; Ft. Apache, P.O. Ft. Apache, Navajo Co, AZ; yes; *(Blank)*
767; Edith; f; 11 (1921); F; s; dau; yes; yes; *(Blank)*
768; Zinco; f; 7 (1925); F; s; dau; yes; yes; 230
769; Si He; f; 5 (1927); F; s; dau; yes; yes; 231
770; Denna Guy; m; 3 (1929); F; s; son; yes; yes; 85

771; Charley John; m; 27 (1905); F; m; Head; yes; yes; 142
772; Big John Bitse; f; 24 (1908); F; m; wife; yes; yes; 105
773; As Soie Bah; f; 7 (1925); F; s; dau; yes; yes; 111
774; Sew Bah; f; 9 (1923); F; s; dau; yes; yes; 915
775; Ye Gos Bah; f; 4 (1928); F; s; dau; yes; yes; 578

NAVAJO INDIAN CENSUS, (As of April 1, 1932)
KEY: Census Number; Name; Sex; Age at Last Birthday; Tribe (Navajo, unless otherwise stated); Degree of Blood; Marital Status; Relationship to Head of Family; At Jurisdiction where enrolled [Yes or No] (If no, Where); Ward [Yes or No]; Allotment, Annuity, and Identification Numbers.

776; Charley, Sam; m; 35 (1897); F; m; Head; yes; yes; 2828
777; Charley, Lucy; f; 45 (1887); F; m; wife; yes; yes; 2829
778; Maxwell; f; 23 (1909); F; s; ?; yes; yes; 4564

779; Charlie; m; 41 (1891); F; m; Head; yes; yes; 977
780; Yel Ne Bah; f; 22 (1910); F; m; wife; yes; yes; 976
781; Al Na Ha Ge Be; f; 12 (1920); F; s; dau; yes; yes; 3306
782; Zahn; f; 16 (1916); F; s; dau; yes; yes; 3336

783; Chee, Aszan; f; 23 (1909); F; s; Head; yes; yes; 542
784; Hoskie Bahhe; m; 9 (1923); F; s; nephew; yes; yes; 543
785; Bay Ah De La He; m; 14 (1918); F; s; nephew; yes; yes; *(Blank)*

786; Chee Cay; m; 33 (1899); F; m; Head; yes; yes; *(Blank)*
787; Chee Cay's Wife; f; 24 (1908); F; m; wife; yes; yes; 5603
788; Daniel; m; 18 (1914); F; s; bro; yes; yes; *(Blank)*
789; Walthie; m; 18 (1914); F; s; bro; yes; yes; 4405
790; De Net De Cho Li; m; 15 (1917); F; s; bro; yes; yes; 5604
791; Yazza Aszan; f; 13 (1919); F; s; sis; yes; yes; 5613

792; Chee Cay Bega; m; 66 (1866); F; m; Head; yes; yes; 5605
793; She Cay Benna; f; 33 (1899); F; m; wife; yes; yes; 5606

794; Cheesee Na Ana Bega; m; 29 (1903); F; m; Head; yes; yes; 3777
795; Cheesee Ana's Wife; f; 19 (1913); F; m; wife; yes; yes; 3773
796; Bahhe; m; 16 (1916); F; s; bro; yes; yes; *(Blank)*
797; Zahn Ta Lea; f(?); 9 (1923); F; s; bro(?); yes; yes; *(Blank)*
798; Bah Ki So; f; 7 (1925); F; s; dau; yes; yes; *(Blank)*
799; Ah Sha He; f; 5 (1927); F; s; dau; yes; yes; 3774
800; Denna Socie; f; 3 (1929); F; s; dau; yes; yes; 3775

801; Cheesee Nanna Bega #2; m; 28 (1904); F; m; Head; yes; yes; *(Blank)*
802; Aszan Gay; f; 25 (1907); F; m; wife; yes; yes; 3776

803; Che The Chize Ne; f; 82 (1850); F; w; Head; yes; yes; 4488
804; Way Bahhe; f; 14 (1918); F; s; dau; yes; yes; 4489
805; Kee Tolle; m; 4 (1928); F; s; son; yes; yes; 4472

806; Chee Zini, Hosteen; m; 38 (1894); F; m; Head; yes; yes; 850
807; Soise Bema; f; 33 (1899); F; m; wife; yes; yes; 813
809; Si Si; m; 11 (1921); F; s; son; yes; yes; 1397
810; Gle Des Bah; m; 7 (1925); F; s; son; yes; yes; 814
811; Gee; m; 6 (1926); F; s; son; yes; yes; 815
812; Seginey Begay; m; 23 (1909) F; s; ?; yes; yes; *(Blank)*

NAVAJO INDIAN CENSUS, (As of April 1, 1932)

KEY: Census Number; Name; Sex; Age at Last Birthday; Tribe (Navajo, unless otherwise stated); Degree of Blood; Marital Status; Relationship to Head of Family; At Jurisdiction where enrolled [Yes or No] (If no, Where); Ward [Yes or No]; Allotment, Annuity, and Identification Numbers.

813; Ye Da Hes Bema; f; 27 (1905); F; s; ?; yes; yes; 816
814; Ye Da Hes Bah; f; 6 (1926); F; s; ?; yes; yes; 817
815; Ye Tas Bah; m; 5 (1927); F; s; son; yes; yes; 818
816; Ye Da He Lo Wood; m; 23 (1909); F; s; ?; yes; yes; 1393
817; Ye Ne Yaz; m; 17 (1915); F; s; ?; yes; yes; *(Blank)*
818; Alice; f; 11 (1921); F; s; ?; no; Ft. Defiance, P.O. Ft. Defiance, Navajo Co, AZ; yes; *(Blank)*
819; Da Yazzie; f; 3 (1929); F; s; dau; yes; yes; 1396
   (NOTE: #808 was omitted from original)

820; Chet Chilli Yet Toe, Hosteen; m; 43 (1889); F; m; Head; yes; yes; 306
821; Hosteen Gann Bitse #1; f; 38 (1894); F; m; wife; yes; yes; 309
822; Dina Yazza; m; 10 (1922); F; s; son; yes; yes; 305
823; Bahs Ne Wah; f; 7 (1925); F; s; dau; yes; yes; 307
824; Dis Wood; m; 5 (1927); F; s; son; yes; yes; 308

825; Chizzy Nez Badoni; m; 50 (1882); F; m; Head; yes; yes; 2969
826; Chizzy Nez Bitsi; f; 33 (1899); F; m; wife; yes; yes; *(Blank)*
827; Eli; m; 20 (1912); F; s; son; no; Truxton Canyon, P.O. Valentine, Mojave Co, AZ; yes; *(Blank)*
828; Bizah Haloni; m; 13 (1919); F; s; son; yes; yes; 2970
829; Hosteen Deel; m; 8 (1924); F; s; son; yes; yes; 2971
830; Ah Aye Baahe; f; 6 (1926); F; s; dau; yes; yes; 2972

831; Chizzy Ua Billy; m; 33 (1899); F; m; Head; yes; yes; *(Blank)*
832; Chizzy Ua Billy's Wife; f; 58 (1874); F; m; wife; yes; yes; *(Blank)*
833; Way He; f; 11 (1921); F; s; dau; yes; yes; *(Blank)*

834; Chizzy Uah Billy Badoni; m; 28 (1904); F; m; Head; yes; yes; *(Blank)*
835; Chizzy's Daughter; f; 19 (1913); F; m; wife; yes; yes; 3907
836; Yazzie Hoskie; m; 3 (1929); F; s; son; yes; yes; 3906

837; Ch Le Bahhe Bitsone; m; ?; F; m; Head; yes; yes; *(Blank)*
838; Ah De Chi Socie Bitsie; f; 20 (1912); F; m; wife; yes; yes; 4229
840; Jah Ye; m; 19 (1913); F; s; son; yes; yes; *(Blank)*
841; Elmer; m; 17 (1915); F; s; son; yes; yes; *(Blank)*
842; Has Bah; f; 5 (1927); F; s; dau; yes; yes; 4230
   (NOTE: #839 was omitted from original)

843; Chosie Ci Benna; f; 26 (1906); F; w; Head; yes; yes; 6037
844; Can; f; 15 (19170; F; s; stp-dau; yes; yes; 6061
845; Chosie Si; m; 9 (1923); F; s; son; yes; yes; 6038
846; Aszan Soi; f; 4 (1928); F; s; dau; yes; yes; 4106

NAVAJO INDIAN CENSUS, (As of April 1, 1932)

KEY: Census Number; Name; Sex; Age at Last Birthday; Tribe (Navajo, unless otherwise stated); Degree of Blood; Marital Status; Relationship to Head of Family; At Jurisdiction where enrolled [Yes or No] (If no, Where); Ward [Yes or No]; Allotment, Annuity, and Identification Numbers.

847; Ch Skizzy Bega; m; 49 (1883); F; m; Head; yes; yes; 740
848; Ja Nas Bah; f; 29 (1903); F; m; wife; yes; yes; 741
849; Zani; f; 23 (1909); F; s; dau; yes; yes; 742
850; Zahn Socie, Jo Ann; f; 10 (1922); F; s; dau; yes; yes; 1631

851; Cisco; m; ?; F; m; Head; yes; yes; 4052
852; Cisco's Wife; f; ?; F; m; wife; yes; yes; 3590

853; Cisse Nez Bega; m; 27 (1905); F; w; Head; yes; yes; 5755
854; Cisse Zan; m; 5 (1927); F; s; son; yes; yes; 5749
855; Banna Soi; m; 21 (1911); F; s; bro; yes; yes; 5750
856; Zahn Soi; f; 17 (1915); F; s; sis; yes; yes; 5751
857; Ze Nez; m; 14 (1918); F; s; bro; yes; yes; *(Blank)*

858; Clah; m; ?; F; m; Head; yes; yes; 972
859; Ah Cayne Bah; f; ?; F; m; wife; yes; yes; 530
860; Kee Si He; m; 6 (1926); F; s; son; yes; yes; 531

861; Clah m; 53 (1879); F; m; Head; yes; yes; 3501
862; Na Ne Bah; f; 33 (1899); F; m; wife; yes; yes; 3539
863; Ah Kee Da Bah; f; 19 (1913); F s; dau; yes; yes; 3538
864; Ne Bah; f; 8 (1924); F; s; dau; yes; yes; 3537

865; Clah; m; 43 (1889); F; w; Head; yes; yes; 4271
866; Toe Ne; m; 12 (1920); F; s; son; yes; yes; *(Blank)*
867; Kee Si He; m; 9 (1923); F; s; son; yes; yes; *(Blank)*
868; Kee Bahhe; m; 7 (1925); F; s; son; yes; yes; 4274
869; Glic Yazza; f; 5 (1927); F; s; dau; yes; yes; 4287
870; Chilli, Teddy; m; 3 (1929); F; s; son; yes; yes; 4275

871; Clah, Aszan; f; ?; F; w; Head; yes; yes; 61
872; Hazel; f; 18 (1914); F; s; dau; yes; yes; 65
873; Soi He; f; 11 (1921); F; s; dau; yes; yes; 46
874; Zani Si He; f; 6 (1926); F; s; dau; yes; yes; 49

875; Clah, James; m; 52 (1880); F; m; Head; yes; yes; 3739
876; Bah; f; 29 (1903); F; m; wife; yes; yes; 3740
877; Mahme; m; 12 (1920); F; s; son; yes; yes; 3747
878; Aszanne Ade Aga; f; 9 (1923); F; s; dau; yes; yes; 3748
879; Catholic; m; 7 (1925); F; s; son; yes; yes; 3741
880; Yah Be Bahhe; m; 3 (1929); F; s; son; yes; yes; 3742

881; Clah, John King; m; 27 (1905); F; m; Head; yes; yes; 1456

NAVAJO INDIAN CENSUS, (As of April 1, 1932)

KEY: Census Number; Name; Sex; Age at Last Birthday; Tribe (Navajo, unless otherwise stated); Degree of Blood; Marital Status; Relationship to Head of Family; At Jurisdiction where enrolled [Yes or No] (If no, Where); Ward [Yes or No]; Allotment, Annuity, and Identification Numbers.

882; Clah Ah Ne Ne; m; ?; F; m; Head; yes; yes; 4028
883; Bahas Zan; f; 38 (1894); F; m; wife; yes; yes; 4029
884; Yazza, May; f; 17 (1915); F; s; dau; yes; yes; 4030
885; Harry; m; 14 (1918); F; s; son; yes; yes; 4031
886; Homer; m; 12 (1920); F; s; son; yes; yes; 4032
887; Zahnie Goy; f; 10 (1922); F; s; dau; yes; yes; 4033
888; Kee Ath Ye; m; 4 (1928); F; s; son; yes; yes; 4406
889; Aszan Socie; f; ?; F; m; wife; #2; yes; yes; 4034

890; Clah Klinny; m; 48 (1884); F; m; Head; yes; yes; 55
891; Hosteen Schene Bitse #1; f; 48 (1884); F; m; wife; yes; yes; 32
892; Toli; m; 13 (1919); F; s; son; yes; yes; *(Blank)*

893; Clah's Son; m; 33 (1899); F; m; Head; yes; yes; 3521
894; Clah's Son's Wife; f; 23 (1909); F; m; wife; yes; yes; 3520
895; Socie Clizzy Klanny; m; 5 (1927); F; s; son; yes; yes; 3522
896; Yazza, Harold; m; 15 (1917); F; s; bro-in-law; yes; yes; 3345

897; Clah Yazza; m; 33 (1899); F; m; Head; yes; yes; 3367
898; Way Si He; f; 35 (1897); F; m; wife; yes; yes; 3368
899; Si Licht Bahhe; f; 11 (1921); F; s; dau; yes; yes; 3369
900; Sh Way; m; 3 (1929); F; s; son; yes; yes; 3371

901; Clanny Zinny Begay; m; 28 (1904); F; w; Head; yes; yes; 4284

902; Clay, Hosteen; m; 26 (1906); F; m; Head; yes; yes; 744
903; De Wazza Bitse; f; 35 (1897); F; m; wife; yes; yes; 743
904; Ethel; f; 14 (1918); F; s; dau; yes; yes; 1303
905; Ye Ne Ah; m; 10 (1922); F; s; son; yes; yes; 745
906; Ne Cay Bah; f; 8 (1924); F; s; dau; yes; yes; 746
907; Kee Yazze; m; 5 (1927); F; s; son; yes; yes; 747

908; Clay Yazze; m; 34 (1898); F; w; Head; yes; yes; *(Blank)*
909; Yah Si; m; 15 (1917); F; s; son; yes; yes; *(Blank)*
910; Kee; m; 11 (1921); F; s; son; yes; yes; *(Blank)*
911; Ah Tade Toll; f; 7 (1925); F; s; dau; yes; yes; 18
912; Hosk The Ne Yah; m; 3 (1929); D; s; son; yes; yes; 944
913; Lois; f; 20 (1912); F; s; niece; yes; yes; *(Blank)*

914; Cle Bitsey; m; 64 (1868); F; w; Head; yes; yes; *(Blank)*
915; Frank; m; 13 (1919); F; s; son; yes; yes; *(Blank)*
916; Chee Ye Ye; m; 21 (1911); F; s; son; yes; yes; *(Blank)*
917; Jackson, Anita; f; 19 (1913); F; s; dau; yes; yes; 3531
918; Hoskie Nez; m; 4 (1928); F; s; son; yes; yes; 4493

NAVAJO INDIAN CENSUS, (As of April 1, 1932)

KEY: Census Number; Name; Sex; Age at Last Birthday; Tribe (Navajo, unless otherwise stated); Degree of Blood; Marital Status; Relationship to Head of Family; At Jurisdiction where enrolled [Yes or No] (If no, Where); Ward [Yes or No]; Allotment, Annuity, and Identification Numbers.

919; Da Cee; f; 28 (1904); F; s; dau; yes; yes; 3530
920; Bahhe, Ada; f; 3 (1929); F; s; dau; yes; yes; 4494
921; Cle Bah; f; 8 (1924); F; s; dau; yes; yes; 3529
922; Bee He; f; 6 (1926); F; s; dau; yes; yes; 2538

923; Clee Chee, Hosteen; m; 65 (1867); F; w; Head; yes; yes; 1135
924; Has Zani; f; 19 (1913); F; s; grnd-dau; yes; yes; 767
925; Chee Ne, George; m; 13 (1919) F; s; grnd-son; yes; yes; *(Blank)*
926; Kee; m; 8 (1924); F; s; grnd-son; yes; yes; 768
927; Aszan Socie; f; 17 (1915); F; s; grnd-dau; yes; yes; *(Blank)*

928; Cle Chee Beds, Hosteen; m; ?; F; w; Head; yes; yes; 1138
929; Bega, Denny; m; ?; F; s; son; no; Ft. Apache, P.O. Ft. Apache, Apache Co, AZ; yes; 1128
930; Billy, John; m; 24 (1908); F; s; son; yes; yes; 396

931; Cle Ha Bah; f; 43 (1889); F; w; Head; yes; yes; 2910
932; Cle Ha Bah, Sevina; f; 17 (1915); F; s; dau; yes; yes; *(Blank)*
933; Soi Ze; m; 10 (1922); F; s; son; yes; yes; *(Blank)*
934; Aszan Ta Ne Zahne; f; ?; F; w; grnd-mother; yes; yes; *(Blank)*

935; Cle Zinny, Hosteen; m; 81 (1851); F; m; Head; yes; yes; 545
936; Aszan Nez; f; 44 (1888); F; m; wife; yes; yes; 544
937; De Na Soi, Alvin; m; 18 (1914); F; s; son; yes; yes; 546
938; Do Yazze; f; 12 (1920); F; s; dau; yes; yes; 547
939; Ada; f; 16 (1916); F; s; dau; yes; yes; 965

940; Clizzie Thane; m; 56 (1876); F; m; Head; yes; yes; 2469
941; Clizzie Thane's Wife; f; 51 (1881); F; m; wife; yes; yes; 2470
942; Waychee, Winifred; f; 20 (1912); F; s; dau; yes; yes; 2471
943; Ada; f; 13 (1919); F; s; dau; yes; yes; 2472
944; Chee, Augusta; f; 10 (1922); F; s; dau; yes; yes; 2473

945; Clizzy; f; 22 (1922); F; s; Head; yes; yes; *(Blank)*
946; Aszan; f; 8 (1924); F; s; sis; yes; yes; 2859

947; Clizzy De Seayye Goat Skins; m; 38 (1894); F; m; yes; yes; 3042
948; Bah; f; 35 (1897); F; m; wife; yes; yes; 5872
949; Na Soi He; f; 15 (19170; F; s; dau; yes; yes; 6085
950; Aszan Le Zinney; f; 13 (1919) F; s; dau; yes; yes; 5873
951; Askie; m; 6 (1926); F; s; son; yes; yes; 5874
952; Ah Bae; f; 3 (1929); F; s; dau; yes; yes; 6081

NAVAJO INDIAN CENSUS, (As of April 1, 1932)
KEY: Census Number; Name; Sex; Age at Last Birthday; Tribe (Navajo, unless otherwise stated); Degree of Blood; Marital Status; Relationship to Head of Family; At Jurisdiction where enrolled [Yes or No] (If no, Where); Ward [Yes or No]; Allotment, Annuity, and Identification Numbers.

953; Clizzy Clanny; m; 33 (1899); F; m; Head; yes; yes; 5912
954; Clizzy Clanny Bay Aszan; f; 30 (1902); F; m; wife; yes; yes; 5913
955; Nez; f; 14 (1918); F; s; dau; yes; yes; 4557
956; Marie; f; 11 (1921); F; s; dau; yes; yes; 5914
957; Na Chi Chee; m; 5 (1927); F; s; son; yes; yes; 4558
958; Hoskie Guy; m; 4 (1928); F; s; son; yes; yes; 5915
959; Zahn Kai; f; 3 (1929); F; s; dau; yes; yes; 4556

960; Clizzy Clanny, Aszan; f; 53 (1879); F; w; Head; yes; yes; *(Blank)*

961; Clizzy Clanny, Aszan; f; 65 (1867); F; w; Head; yes; yes; 5917
962; Hosteen Be Da Ah Clanny; m; 26 (1906); F; s; son; yes; yes; 5918
963; Aszan Clizzy; f; 10 (1922); F; s; dau; yes; yes; 5919
964; Richard Long; m; 25 (1907); F; s; son; yes; yes; 5920

965; Clizzy Klanny, Joe; m; 30 (1902); F; m; Head; yes; yes; 3750
966; Hoskie Ha Ye Zen Bit Sui; f; 26 (1906); F; m; wife; yes; yes; 3737
967; Cleo; f; 10 (1922); F; s; dau; yes; yes; 3736
968; Guy; m; 7 (1925); F; s; son; yes; yes; 3738
969; Edgar Miller; m; 24 (1908); F; s; bro L[sic]; yes; yes; 1141
970; Be Ho Zone Ne; f; 4 (1928); F; s; dau; yes; yes; 1140

971; Clizzy Tanne, Hosteen; m; 65 (1867); F; m; Head; yes; yes; *(Blank)*
972; Hosteen Clizzy Thane's Wife; f; 61 (1871); F; m; wife; yes; yes; *(Blank)*
973; Wince; f; 21 (1911); F; s; dau; yes; yes; *(Blank)*
974; Ah Adie; f; 13 (1919); F; s; dau; yes; yes; *(Blank)*
975; Sisce; f; 11 (1921); F; s; dau; yes; yes; *(Blank)*
976; Ked Niche; f; 20 (1912); F; s; dau; yes; yes; *(Blank)*

977; Clony Zinni; m; ?; F; m; Head; yes; yes; 574
978; Mary Ellen; f; 38 (1894); F; m; wife; yes; yes; 220
979; Yazze, Grace; f; 20 (1912); F; s; dau; yes; yes; 214
980; Yazze, Nora; f; 19 (1913); F; s; dau; yes; yes; 215
981; Hardy, David; m; 16 (1916); F; s; son; no; Ft. Apache, P.O. Ft. Apache, Navajo Co, AZ; 574
982; Dick; m; 13 (1919); F; s; son; no; Ft. Apache, P.O. Ft. Apache, Navajo Co, AZ; 1322
983; Hardy, Guy; m; 9 (1923); F; s; son; yes; yes; 1323
984; Philip; m; 7 (1925); F; s; son; yes; yes; 216
985; Roger; m; 6 (1926); F; s; son; yes; yes; 217
986; Bahhe; m; 5 (1927); F; s; son; yes; yes; 218
987; Bessie; f; 3 (1929); F; s; dau; yes; yes; 1320
988; Elsie; f; 3 (1929); F; s; dau; yes; yes; 1321
989; Aye Yazze; f; 4 (1928); F; s; grnd-dau; yes; yes; 219

NAVAJO INDIAN CENSUS, (As of April 1, 1932)

KEY: Census Number; Name; Sex; Age at Last Birthday; Tribe (Navajo, unless otherwise stated); Degree of Blood; Marital Status; Relationship to Head of Family; At Jurisdiction where enrolled [Yes or No] (If no, Where); Ward [Yes or No]; Allotment, Annuity, and Identification Numbers.

990; Closi, Hosteen; m; 62 (1870); F; m; Head; yes; yes; 2957
991; Closi's, Hosteen, Wife; f; 51 (1881); F; m; wife; yes; yes; 2435
992; Kai, Ada; f; 4 (1928); F; s; dau; yes; yes; 2436
993; Ye De Bah, Bessie Rope; f; 3 (1929); F; s; dau; yes; yes; 2432

994; Cloth Be Nelly #2, Aszan; m; 29 (1903); F; m; Head; yes; yes; *(Blank)*
995; Zahn Nue Bahhe; f; 35 (1897); F; m; wife; yes; yes; 3738
996; Bah Ha; f; 19 (1913); F; s; dau; yes; yes; *(Blank)*
997; Tolea; m; 8 (1924); F; s; son; yes; yes; *(Blank)*
998; Zahn Ah See; f; 8 (1924); F; s; dau; yes; yes; 3779
999; Zahn Nie See He; f; 8 (1924); F; s; dau; yes; yes; 3780
1000; Soha Hoskie; m; 4 (1928); F; s; son; yes; yes; 3781

1001; Cow Boy, m; 58 (1874); F; m; Head; yes; yes; 3908
1002; Cow Boy's Wife; f; ?; F; m; wife; yes; yes; 3914
1003; Kee; m; 18 (1914); F; s; son; yes; yes; 3913
1004; Lilly; f; 15 (1917); F; s; dau; yes; yes; 3909
1005; Cle Ge; m; 11 (1921); F; s; son; yes; yes; 3910
1006; Do She; m; 8 (1924); F; s; son; yes; yes; 3911
1007; Zonnie; m; 7 (1925); F; s; son; yes; yes; 3912

1008; Con Hosk; m; 48 (1884); F; m; Head; yes; yes; 3518
1009; Con's Wife; f; 38 (1894); F; m; wife; yes; yes; 3516
1010; Yazza, Roma; f; 20 (1912); F; s; dau; yes; yes; 3617
1011; Mahaz; m; 15 (1917); F; s; son; yes; yes; 3515
1012; Jennie; f; 12 (1920); F; s; dau; yes; yes; 4428
1013; Norma; f; 8 (1924); F; s; dau; yes; yes; 3514
1014; Sam; m; 5 (1927); F; s; son; yes; yes; 3513
1015; Bahhe Na Zoing; f; 3 (1929); F; s; dau; yes; yes; 4427

1016; Con Soi Hosh; m; 73 (1859); F; w; Head; yes; yes; 6342

1017; Cook, Jim; m; ?; F; m; Head; yes; yes; 89
1018; Jim's Wife; f; 37 (1895); F; m; wife; yes; yes; 188
1019; Harry; m; 22 (1910); F; s; son; yes; yes; *(Blank)*
1020; Ye Li Wood; m; 20 (192); F; s; son; yes; yes; 929
1021; Kan; f; 13 (1919); F; s; dau; yes; yes; 189
1022; Cook, John; m; 17 (1915); F; s; son; yes; yes; 924
1023; Ah Tahe Bahhe, Alice; f; 15 (1917); F; s; dau; no; Ft. Apache, P.O. Ft. Apache, Navajo Co, AZ; yes; 925
1024; Ah Chee Bah Ho Zoni; m; 10 (1922); F; s; son; yes; yes; 930
1025; Bah; f; 8 (1924); F; s; dau; yes; yes; 190
1026; Se Chee He; m; 6 (1926); F; s; son; yes; yes; 191
1027; Dis Bah; f; 5 (1927); F; s; dau; yes; yes; 192

NAVAJO INDIAN CENSUS, (As of April 1, 1932)

KEY: Census Number; Name; Sex; Age at Last Birthday; Tribe (Navajo, unless otherwise stated); Degree of Blood; Marital Status; Relationship to Head of Family; At Jurisdiction where enrolled [Yes or No] (If no, Where); Ward [Yes or No]; Allotment, Annuity, and Identification Numbers.

1028; Ye Ne Tahe; f; 4 (1928); F; s; dau; yes; yes; 926

1029; Cook, John; m; 3 (1899); F; m; Head; yes; yes; 486
1030; Aszan Ye Glo He; f; 48 (1884); F; m; wife; yes; yes; 487
1031; Chee; m; 15 (1917); F; s; bro; yes; yes; 503
1032; Billy, John; m; 28 (1904); F; s; stp-son; yes; yes; 502

1033; Cowboy's Sister; f; 58 (1874); F; w; Head; yes; yes; 4011
1034; No Soi; m; 23 (1909); F; s; son; yes; yes; *(Blank)*
1035; Selma; f; 10 (1922); F; s; dau; yes; yes; 4000
1036; Jinny Schon; m; 20 (1912); F; s; son; yes; yes; 4004
1037; Minnie; f; 13 (1919); F; s; dau; yes; yes; 4001
1038; Dolea; f; 8 (1924); F; s; dau; yes; yes; 4003

1039; Crooked finger; m; 85 (1847); F; m; Head; yes; yes; 3916
1040; Crooked Finger's Wife; f; 81 (1851); F; m; wife; yes; yes; 3859
1041; Johnnie; m; 21 (1911); F; s; grnd-son; yes; yes; 3860
1042; Aszan Zon; f; 16 (1916); F; s; grnd-dau; yes; yes; 3862
1043; Yazzie; m; 11 (1921); F; s; grnd-son; yes; yes; 3861
1044; Socie; m; 9 (1923); F; s; grnd-son; yes; yes; 4430
1045; Olch Tihe; m; 9 (1923); F; s; grnd-son; yes; yes; *(Blank)*
1046; Bah Ye Ne; f; 4 (1928); F; s; grnd-dau; yes; yes; 3863
1047; Ye Aye Zaht Hoskie; m; 6 (1926); F; s; grnd-son; yes; yes; 4431

1048; Crooked Finger's Grand-son; m; 24 (1908); F; m; Head; yes; yes; 3841
1049; Gee Hal Bitsey; f; 27 (1905); F; m; wife; yes; yes; 3842
1050; Yazza De Nez, Jack; m; 13 (1919); F; s; nephew; yes; yes; 3843

1051; Da Bitsoni Goody; m; ?; F; m; Head; yes; yes; 2407
1052; Da Bitsoni Goody's Wife; f; ?; F; m; wife; yes; yes; 2408
1053; Na La Yezzie; m; 3 (1929); F; s; son; yes; yes; 2491

1054; Daf Ah She No; m; 53 (1879); F; m; Head; yes; yes; 3672
1055; Dah Ah She Ne's Wife; f; 43 (1889); F; m; wife; yes; yes; 3673
1056; Bruce; m; 16 (1916); F; s; son; yes; yes; 3677
1057; Bahhe Ah Ade; f; 13 (1919); F; s; dau; yes; yes; 3674
1058; Chee; m; 11 (1921); F; s; son; yes; yes; 3675
1059; Chee Nadah; m; 9 (1923); F; s; son; yes; yes; 3676
1060; Yazzie Kee; m; 6 (1926); F; s; son; yes; yes; 3678
1061; Socie Wes; m; 3 (1929); F; s; son; yes; yes; 3679
1062; Lucille; f; 12 (1920); F; s; dau; yes; yes; 3684
1063; Way She He; m; 2 (1930); F; s; son; yes; yes; 4501

NAVAJO INDIAN CENSUS, (As of April 1, 1932)
KEY: Census Number; Name; Sex; Age at Last Birthday; Tribe (Navajo, unless otherwise stated); Degree of Blood; Marital Status; Relationship to Head of Family; At Jurisdiction where enrolled [Yes or No] (If no, Where); Ward [Yes or No]; Allotment, Annuity, and Identification Numbers.

1064; Daffy, Mike; m; 33 (1899); F; m; Head; yes; yes; 1103
1065; Bah, f; 25 (1927); F; m; wife; yes; yes; 16
1066; Zahns Soi; f; 14 (1918); F; s; niece; yes; yes; 1104
1067; Dennet Bahhe, Pedro; m; 13 (1919); F; s; nephew; no; Ft. Wingate, P.O. Wingate, NM; yes; 1105

1068; Da Has Bah; f; 47 (1885); f; w; Head; yes; yes; 3743
1069; Morgan, Dan; m; 18 (1914); F; s; son; yes; yes; 3744
1070; Morgan, Clinton; m; 12 (1920); F; s; son; yes; yes; 3745
1071; Hoskie Bahhe; m; 4 (1928); F; s; son; yes; yes; 3746
1072; Chee; f; 8 (1924); F; s; dau; yes; yes; 3749

1073; Dah La Than Ne; m; 42 (1890); F; m; Head; yes; yes; 5842
1074; Lona Zon Bitsi; f; 32 (1900); F; m; wife; yes; yes; 5843
1075; Dennet She Ne Gah; m; 3 (1929); F; s; son; yes; yes; *(Blank)*
*1077; Dennea Sini Gate He; m; 3 (1929); F; s; son; yes; yes; 6077

1078; Zahn Kili, Madge; f; 17 (1915); F; m; wife; yes; yes; 5844
1079; Hollywood, Mark; m; 16 (1916); F; s; son; yes; yes; 6075
         (*NOTE: #1076 omitted from original)

1080; Dan Yazza's Wife; f; 29 (1903); F; w; Head; yes; yes; 5685
1081; Socie; m; 11 (1921); F; s; son; yes; yes; 5686
1081; Yazza Bah; f; 9 (1923); F; s; dau; yes; yes; 5687
1082; Socie Yazza; m; 8 (1924); F; s; son; yes; yes; 5688
1083; As He De Bah; f; 4 (1928); F; s; dau; yes; yes; 5689

1084; Da La Nezzie; m; ?; F; m; Head; yes; yes; *(Blank)*
1085; Ah Ha Gee Bah; f; ?; F; m; wife; yes; yes; 1488
1086; Harrison; m; 18 (1914); F; s; son; yes; yes; 1608
1087; Dewey; m; 18 (1914); F; s; nephew; yes; yes; *(Blank)*
1088; Luke; m; 18 (1914); F; s; nephew; yes; yes; 1645
1089; Way Bahhe; f; 9 (1923); F; s; dau; yes; yes; 1489
1090; Bitone Chee; m; 3 (1929); F; s; son; yes; yes; 1639

1091; Dan; m; ?; F; m; Head; yes; yes; *(Blank)*
1092; Has Bah; f; 20 (1912); F; m; wife; yes; yes; 897
1093; Ah Pade Yazza; f; 4 (1928); F; s; dau; yes; yes; 898
1094; Hoskie; m; 2 (1930); F; s; son; yes; yes; 1398

1095; Dase, Aszan; f; 75 (1857); F; w; Head; yes; yes; 4483
1096; Kee Ha Das Bah, Ada; f; 19 (1913); F; s; grnd-dau; yes; yes; 4484

1097; Da Va Chee; m; 33 (1899); F; w; Head; yes; yes; 3944

NAVAJO INDIAN CENSUS, (As of April 1, 1932)

KEY: Census Number; Name; Sex; Age at Last Birthday; Tribe (Navajo, unless otherwise stated); Degree of Blood; Marital Status; Relationship to Head of Family; At Jurisdiction where enrolled [Yes or No] (If no, Where); Ward [Yes or No]; Allotment, Annuity, and Identification Numbers.

1098; Da Va He; m; 53 (1879); F; m; Head; yes; yes; *(Blank)*
1099; Aszan Sanne Toe He; f; 77 (1855); F; m; wife; yes; yes; 1585

1100; Da Va Socie; m; 35 (1897); F; m; Head; yes; yes; *(Blank)*
1101; Soni Sotsis, Martha; f; 29 (1903); F; m; wife; yes; yes; 1528
1102; Chee; m; 9 (1923); F; s; son; yes; yes; 1529
1103; Ta Nah Bah; f; 8 (1924); F; s; dau; yes; yes; 1530
1104; Kee Ah Si Ne; m; 5 (1927); F; s; son; yes; yes; 1531
1105; Andrews, George; m; 3 (1929); F; s; son; yes; yes; 1532

1106; Da Va Socie; m; 53 (1879); F; m; Head; yes; yes; 2958
1107; Da Va Socie's Wife; f; 32 (1900); F; m; wife; yes; yes; 2959
1108; Paddock, Anthony; m; 24 (1908); F; s; son; yes; yes; 2960
1109; Ralph; m; 18 (1914); F; s; son; yes; yes; 2474
1110; Way Showie; f; 15 (1917); F; s; dau; yes; yes; 2475
1111; Nah; f; 13 (1919); F; s; dau; yes; yes; 2477
1112; Yazze; m; 10 (1922); F; s; son; yes; yes; 2476
1113; Ah Aye Yazze; f; 4 (1928); F; s; dau; yes; yes; 2962

1114; Dayate, She Bega She; f; 25 (1907); F; w; Head; yes; yes; 6406

1115; Dead Horse; m; 45 (1887); F; m; Head; yes; yes; 3949
1116; Crooked Finger's Daughter #3; f; 43 (1889); F; m; wife; yes; yes; 3950
1117; De Jole; m; 20 (1912); F; s; son; yes; yes; *(Blank)*
1118; Wilson; m; 17 (1915); F; s; son; yes; yes; 4434
1119; Glenie Bah; f; 9 (1923); F; s; dau; yes; yes; 3931
1120; Ye He Bah; f; 4 (1928); F; s; dau; yes; yes; 4433

1121; De Cho Li; m; 33 (1899); F; m; Head; yes; yes; *(Blank)*
1122; Ayede; f; 25 (1907); F; m; wife; yes; yes; 156
1123; Bah He; f; 20 (1912); F; s; ?; yes; yes; 158

1124; De Cho Li Bema Hosteen; f; 68 (1864); F; w; Head; yes; yes; 810

1125; Deel, Hosteen; m; 69 (1863); F; m; Head; yes; yes; 3657
1126; Deel's. Hosteen. Wife #1; f; 43 (1889); F; m; wife; yes; yes; 3685

1127; Deel, Hosteen; m; 41 (1891); F; m; Head; yes; yes; 6425
1128; Deel, Hosteen; f; 33 (1899); F; m; wife; yes; yes; 6426
1129; Deel Begay, Hosteen; m; 18 (1914); F; s; son; yes; yes; 6430
1130; Aszan; f; 7 (1925); F; s; dau; yes; yes; 6419

1131; Deel Begay #3, Hosteen; m; 31 (1901); F; m; Head; yes; yes; 3666
1132; Deel Begay, Hosteen, Wife; f; 28 (1904) F; m; wife; yes; yes; 3658

NAVAJO INDIAN CENSUS, (As of April 1, 1932)

KEY: Census Number; Name; Sex; Age at Last Birthday; Tribe (Navajo, unless otherwise stated); Degree of Blood; Marital Status; Relationship to Head of Family; At Jurisdiction where enrolled [Yes or No] (If no, Where); Ward [Yes or No]; Allotment, Annuity, and Identification Numbers.

1133; Shay; m; 7 (1925); F; s; son; yes; yes; 3659
1134; Zah Chee; f; 6 (1926); F; s; dau; yes; yes; 3660
1135; Ash Kee Bahhe; m; 4 (1928); F; s; son; yes; yes; 3661
1136; Silver Hat Band's Wife #2; f; 29 (1903); F; m; wife; yes; yes; 3662
1137; Bah; f; 9 (1923); F; s; dau; yes; yes; 3663
1138; Socie; f; 7 (1925); F; s; dau; yes; yes; 3664
1139; Beck, Clifford; m; 27 (1905); F; s; ?; yes; yes; *(Blank)*
1140; Sonnie; f; 18 (1914); F; s; dau; yes; yes; 3683

1141; De Joly Denna; m; 60 (1872); F; m; Head; yes; yes; 4020
1142; De Joly Denna's Wife; f; 53 (1879); F; m; wife; yes; yes; 4015
1143; Zahnnie; f; ?; F; s; dau; yes; yes; 4013
1144; De Na So Denny; m; 16 (1916); F; s; son; yes; yes; 4019
1145; Ken; f; 13 (1919); F; s; dau; yes; yes; 4014
1146; So See; f; 11 (1921); F; s; dau; yes; yes; 4016
1147; Ah Ade Soe He; f; 5 (1927); F; s; dau; yes; yes; 4017

1148; De Len Se Jinny; m; ?; F; w; Head; yes; yes; *(Blank)*
1149; Zahn Se He; f; 15 (1917); F; s; dau; yes; yes; 5824
1150; Soie Ahway; f; 13 (1919); F; s; dau; yes; yes; 5641
1151; Yo He, Woody; m; 11 (1921); F; s; son; yes; yes; 5828
1152; Ald Zith Si Ho; m; 6 (1926); F; s; son; yes; yes; 5642
1153; Aske; m; 4 (1928); F; s; son; yes; yes; 5640
1154; Cher Ken; f; 42 (1890); F; m; wife; #2; yes; yes; 4551
1155; Zonnie; f; 20 (1912); F; s; dau; yes; yes; 4552

1156; Dena Ah Ne; m; 67 (1865); F; m; Head; yes; yes; 506
1157; Aszan Chee; f; 43 (1889); F; m; wife; yes; yes; 430
1158; Hosteen Yazze, Abraham; m; 25 (1907); F; s; son; yes; yes; *(Blank)*

1159; Dena Ah Si m; 32 (1900); F; m; Head; yes; yes; 1438
1160; Yah Na Bah; f; ?; F; m; wife; yes; yes; 1439
1161; Bah Soi; f; ?; F; m; wife; yes; yes; 1440

1162; Dena Chilli Be Kis; m; 20 (1912); F; s; Head; yes; yes; *(Blank)*
1163; Hoskie; m; ?; F; s; bro; yes; yes; 2898
1164; Ba Socie; m; 7 (1925); F; s; bro; yes; yes; 2889
1165; Kee Buy; m; 5 (1927); F; s; bro; yes; yes; 2890

1166; Dena De Jole Begay, Mose; m; 33 (1899); F; w; Head; yes; yes; 3589

1167; De Na La Cui; m; 48 (1884); F; m; Head; yes; yes; 3945
1168; De Na La Giu's[sic] Wife; f; 25 (1907); F; m; wife; yes; yes; 3925

NAVAJO INDIAN CENSUS, (As of April 1, 1932)
KEY: Census Number; Name; Sex; Age at Last Birthday; Tribe (Navajo, unless otherwise stated); Degree of Blood; Marital Status; Relationship to Head of Family; At Jurisdiction where enrolled [Yes or No] (If no, Where); Ward [Yes or No]; Allotment, Annuity, and Identification Numbers.

1169; Dena La Guy; m; 64 (1868); F; m; Head; yes; yes; 1444
1170; Dena La Guy's Wife; f; 49 (1883); F; m; wife; yes; yes; 1442
1171; Bahhe, Hosteen; m; 32 (1900); f; s; son; yes; yes; *(Blank)*
1172; Emil; f[sic]; 28 (1904); F; s; son; yes; yes; *(Blank)*
1173; Na Bleen Has Bah; f; 19 (1913); F; s; dau; yes; yes; *(Blank)*
1174; Ye Na Bah; f; 9 (1923); F; s; dau; yes; yes; 1443
1175; Donald; m; 21 (1911); F; s; son; yes; yes; 1613
1176; Howard; m; 28 (1904); F; s; son; yes; yes; 1445

1177; Dena Le Guy Begay; m; 43 (1889); F; m; Head; yes; yes; 1446
1178; Ta Bah Ha De Chi Li Bitsi; f; 34 (1898); F; m; wife; yes; yes; 1447
1179; Sihe; f; 9 (1923); F; s; dau; yes; yes; 1450
1180; Si He Bahhe; f; 7 (1925); F; s; dau; yes; yes; 1451
1181; Denna Bah He; f; 6 (1926); F; s; dau; yes; yes; 1448
1182; Zohn Guy; f; 4 (1928); F; s; dau; yes; yes; 1449
1183; Zinny Bay Aszan; f; ?; F; m; wife; yes; yes; *(Blank)*
1184; Dene Ye Wood Benna; f; 33 (1899); F; s; dau; yes; yes; 1457
1185; Ned; m; 16 (1916); F; s; son; yes; yes; *(Blank)*
1186; Holkie Si Hah Zah; m; 11 (1921); F; s son; yes; yes; 1455
1187; Hoskie Yah Nah Zah; m; ?; F; s; son; yes; yes; *(Blank)*
1188; Bahhe, Ada; f; 2 (1930); F; s; dau; yes; yes; 1625

1189; Dena Nes Bah; f; 48 (1884); F; w; Head; yes; yes; 890
1190; Zoni Yazze; f; 23 (1909); F; w; Dau; yes; yes; 891
1191; Bahn Ne Bah; f; 10 (1922); F; s; grnd-dau; yes; yes; 892
1192; De Si; m; 5 (1927); F; s; grnd-son; yes; yes; 893
1193; Bah Si He; f; 3 (1929); F; s; grnd-dau; yes; yes; 894

1194; Denna Nez; m; ?; F; m; Head; yes; yes; 850
1195; Cay Ne Bah; f; 35 (1897); F; m; wife; yes; yes; 851
1196; Hoskie He Li Wood; m; 14 (1918); F; s; son; no; Ft. Apache, P.O. Ft. Apache; Navajo Co, AZ; yes; 1367
1197; Hoskie Na Hele; m; 7 (1925); F s; son; yes; yes; 852
1198; Hoskie Woody; m; 7 (1925); F; s; son; yes; yes; *(Blank)*

1199; De Na Sea Nava He; m; ?; F; m; Head; yes; yes; 3937
1200; De Ne[sic] Sea Nava He's Wife; f; ?; F; m; wife; yes; yes; 3938

1201; Dena Socie Bega; m; 20 (1912); F; m; Head; yes; yes; *(Blank)*
1202; Aszan Yazze; f; 20 (1912); F; m; wife; yes; yes; 2987
1203; Kee Chee; m; 4 (1928); F; s; son; yes; yes; 3364

1204; Denet Asoises; m; 35 (1897); F; m; Head; yes; yes; 1301
1205; Ruth Ann; f; 33 (1899); F; m; wife; yes; yes; 751

NAVAJO INDIAN CENSUS, (As of April 1, 1932)

KEY: Census Number; Name; Sex; Age at Last Birthday; Tribe (Navajo, unless otherwise stated); Degree of Blood; Marital Status; Relationship to Head of Family; At Jurisdiction where enrolled [Yes or No] (If no, Where); Ward [Yes or No]; Allotment, Annuity, and Identification Numbers.

1206; Kee Chee; m; 6 (1926); F; s; son; yes; yes; 752
1207; Zani Bahhe; f; 5 (1927); F; s; dau; yes; yes; 753
1208; Guy; m; 5 (1927); F; s; son; yes; yes; 754
1209; Ni Glen Ta Ne; f; 3 (1929); F; s; dau; yes; yes; 1302

1210; Denet Bahhe; m; 36 (1896); F; m; Head; yes; yes; 4470
1211; Aszan Yazza; f; 37 (1895); F; m; wife; yes; yes; 4288
1212; Clizzy; m; 27 (1905); F; s; bro; yes; yes; *(Blank)*
1213; Zah Bah, Ruth; f; 15 (1917); F; s; dau; yes; yes; 4471

1214; Denet Da Chee; m; 28 (1904); F; m; Head; yes; yes; 259
1215; Aszan Bahhe; f; 39 (1893); F; m; wife; yes; yes; 238
1216; Aszan De Odie; f; 25 (1907); F; s; ?; yes; yes; *(Blank)*
1217; Dena Sihe; m; 9 (1923); F; s; son; yes; yes; 265
1218; Dena Soi; m; 6 (1926); F; s; son; yes; yes; 239
1219; Soi Yazze; m; 5 (1927); F; s; son; yes; yes; 240
1220; Hoskie Beel; m; 3 (1929); F; s; son; yes; yes; 1178

1221; Denet Socie Bega; m; ?; F; m Head; yes; yes; *(Blank)*
1222; Bema Glee Ha Bah; f; 23 (1909); F; m; wife; yes; yes; 3469
1223; Shati; f; 31 (1901); F; s; dau; yes; yes; 4308
1224; As Hi He Kee; m; 24 (1908); F; s; son; yes; yes; *(Blank)*

1225; Denna Guo; m; 67 (1865); F; m; Head; yes; yes; 1551
1226; Denna Guo's Wife; f; 48 (1884); F; m; wife; yes; yes; 1552
1227; Kee Bahhe; m; 24 (1908); F; s; son; yes; yes; *(Blank)*

1228; Denoc Ah She He; m; 36 (1896); F; m; Head; yes; yes; 6308
1229; Ke To Shia Bitsoni; f; 42 (1890); F; m; wife; yes; yes; 6310
1230; Denoc, Harry; m; 15 (1917); F; s; son; yes; yes; 6486
1231; Bitsie Bitsoni Zahshe He; f; 26 (1906); F; s; sis; yes; yes; 6313
1232; Bitsoni Bahhe; m; 21 (1911); F; s; son; yes; yes; 4504
1233; Sonne; f; 19 (1913); f; s; dau; yes; yes; 6309
1234; Bitsoni Slice, Erick; m; 16 (1916); F; s; son; yes; yes; 6314
1235; Yazza; f; 13 (1919); f; s; dau; yes; yes; 6315
1236; Yazza Kee; m; 9 (1913); F; s; son; yes; yes; 6312
1237; Bahhe She; m; 9 (1923); F; s; grnd-son; yes; yes; *(Blank)*
1238; Bahhe Athle; f; 7 (1925); F; s; grnd-dau; yes; yes; 6311
1239; Little Boy; m; 4 (1928); F; s; grnd-son; yes; yes; *(Blank)*
1240; Sice Kee; m; 4 (1928); F; s; grnd-son; yes; yes; 4509
1241; Kee Sone; m; 5 (1927); F; s; son; yes; yes; 4509

1242; Desbah; m; 90 (1842); F; w; Head; yes; yes; 4208
1243; Si Chil Lie; m; 13 (1919); F; s; son; yes; yes; 4209

NAVAJO INDIAN CENSUS, (As of April 1, 1932)
KEY: Census Number; Name; Sex; Age at Last Birthday; Tribe (Navajo, unless otherwise stated); Degree of Blood; Marital Status; Relationship to Head of Family; At Jurisdiction where enrolled [Yes or No] (If no, Where); Ward [Yes or No]; Allotment, Annuity, and Identification Numbers.

1244; Bah Nal De Bah; f; 6 (19260; F; s; son; yes; yes; 4210

1245; Des Bah; f; 60 (1872); F; w; Head; yes; yes; 4285
1246; Claude; m; 21 (1911); F; s; son; yes; yes; 4473
1257; Bah; f; 12 (1920); F; s; dau; yes; yes; 4286

1248; Desbah; f; 33 (1899); F; w; Head; yes; yes; *(Blank)*
1249; Des Wood; m; 16 (1916); F; s; son; yes; yes; *(Blank)*
1250; Hanibah; f; 10 (1922); F; s; dau; yes; yes; *(Blank)*
1251; Hanesbay; f; 6 (1926); F; s; dau; yes; yes; *(Blank)*
1252; *elah; f; 4 (1928); F; s; dau; yes; yes; *(Blank)*
(*NOTE: Unable to determine the first letter of the name due to strike-over on letter.)

1253; Desyah Tone; m; 61 (1871); F; m; Head; yes; yes; 4531
1254; Bah Yazza; f; 48 (1884); F; m; wife; yes; yes; 4532
1255; Aszan Yazza; f; 26 (1906); F; s; dau; yes; yes; 5847
1256; Nez; f; 9 (1923); F; s; grnd-dau; yes; yes; 5848
1267; Tajachine, Bill; m; 21 (1911); F; s; grnd-son; yes; yes; 4533
1258; Dah Ak Nis Sisi; m; 15 (1917); F; s; grnd-son; yes; yes; 4537
1259; Hade, Charley; m; 12 (1920); F; s; grnd-son; yes; yes; 4539
1260; Bah; f; 9 (1923); F; s; grnd-dau; yes; yes; 4534
1261; Glee Has Bah; f; 7 (1925); F; s; grnd-dau; yes; yes; 4535
1262; Lorenzo Smith; m; 16 (1916); F; s; grnd-son; yes; yes; 5841
1263; Geene, Gus; m; 19 (1913); F; s; grnd-son; yes; yes; 4854

1264; Des Yah Toni Bega; m; 28 (1904); F; w; Head; yes; yes; 5840
1265; Kee Yazza; m; 4 (1928); F; s; son; yes; yes; 5838

1266; De Wizzie Bega; m; 25 (1907); F; m; Head; yes; yes; *(Blank)*
1267; Guy Le; f; 23 (1909); F; m; wife; yes; yes; *(Blank)*

1268; De Wozzie; m; 58 (1874); F; m; Head; yes; yes; 790
1269; Aszan Yazze; f; 53 (1879); F; m; wife; yes; yes; 736

1270; Dina Ani Bega; m; 25 (1907); F; m; Head; yes; yes; 444
1271; Aha Has Bah; f; ?; f; m; wife; yes; yes; 431
1272; Kee Bahhe; m; 4 (1928); F; s; son; yes; yes; 434
1273; Denna Ach He; m; 2 (1930); F; s; son; yes; yes; 920

1274; Detcelia; m; 88 (1844); F; m; Head; yes; yes; 6356
1275; Ket Ce Lia #1 - Wife; f; 52 (1880); F; m; wife; yes; yes; 6365
1276; Ket Ce Lia Wife #2; f; 51 (1881); F; m; wife; yes; yes; 6357
1277; She He; f; 33 (1899); F; w; dau; yes; yes; 6358
1278; Se See; f; 11 (1921); F; s; grnd-dau; yes; yes; 6359

NAVAJO INDIAN CENSUS, (As of April 1, 1932)
KEY: Census Number; Name; Sex; Age at Last Birthday; Tribe (Navajo, unless otherwise stated); Degree of Blood; Marital Status; Relationship to Head of Family; At Jurisdiction where enrolled [Yes or No] (If no, Where); Ward [Yes or No]; Allotment, Annuity, and Identification Numbers.

1279; Dobah Askie; m; 7 (1925); F; s; grnd-son; yes; yes; 6360
1280; Bahhee Aszan; f; 4 (1928); F; s; grnd-dau; yes; yes; 6361

1281; Dinny; m; 28 (1904); F; w; Head; yes; yes; 862

1282; Diny Azhe; m; 41 (1891); F; m; Head; yes; yes; 3921
1283; Bah Ah Yia Bah; f; 39 (1893); F; m; wife; yes; yes; 3820
1284; Dineyazhe, Phillips; f; 18 (1914); F; s; dau; yes; yes; 3821
1285; Dinneyazhe, Allen; m; 15 (1917); F; s; son; yes; yes; 3822
1286; Ruth; f; 12 (1920); F; s; dau; yes; yes; 3824
1287; Willie; m; 10 (1922); F; s; son; yes; yes; 3825
1288; Mary; f; 6 (1926); F; s; dau; yes; yes; 3825
1289; Bah Ah Cia Hinges Bah; f; 10 (1922); F; s; dau; yes; yes; 3827
1290; Hoskie Tole; m; 4 (1928); F; s; son; yes; yes; 970
1291; Denet Le Chee Detchon; m; 25 (1907); F; s; ?; yes; yes; 971
1292; Charlie B: m; ?; F; s; ?; yes; yes; 3828

1293; Do Ah De Si He, Hosteen; m; 93 (1839); F; m; Head; yes; yes; 2841
1294; Aszan Toede Chonne; f; ?; F; m; wife; yes; yes; 2842
1295; Na Dich Ha Done; m; 70 (1862); F; w; son; yes; yes; 2843

1296; Do Choenny; m; 42 (1890); F; m; Head; yes; yes; 4418
1297; Aszan Nez; f; 43 (1889); F; m; wife; yes; yes; 4417
1298; Begay, Harry; m; 23 (1909); F; s; son; yes; yes; 4416
1299; Kenneth; m; 18 (1914); F; s; son; yes; yes; 3548
1300; Bah; f; 16 (1916); F; s; dau; yes; yes; 3549
1301; Aschan Begay; m; 30 (1902); F; s; ?; yes; yes; 3551
1302; Guy; m; 13 (1919); F; s; son; yes; yes; 3552
1303; Chee Hosteen; m; 9 (1923); F; s; son; yes; yes; 3553

1304; Do Ha He, Hosteen; m; 56 (1876); F; w; Head; yes; yes; *(Blank)*
1305; Oth Ta Ye; m; 7 (1925); F; s; son; yes; yes; 4012

1306; Do Has Tahhe; m; 73 (1859); F; w; Head; yes; yes; 3727

1307; Do Ha Tahhe; m; ?; F; m; Head; yes; yes; 2886
1308; Do Ha Tahhe's Wife; f; 29 (1903); F; m; wife; yes; yes; 2879
1309; Kee Nez; m; 9 (1923); F; s; son; yes; yes; 2880
1310; Ken Yazza; f; 6 (1926); F; s; dau; yes; yes; 2881

1311; Do Lee Ho Zonie; m; 53 (1879); F; m; Head; yes; yes; 27
1312; Aszan Soi; f; 36 (1896); F; m; wife; yes; yes; 34
1313; Bays De Bah; f; 9 (1923); F; s; niece; yes; yes; 35

NAVAJO INDIAN CENSUS, (As of April 1, 1932)
KEY: Census Number; Name; Sex; Age at Last Birthday; Tribe (Navajo, unless otherwise stated); Degree of Blood; Marital Status; Relationship to Head of Family; At Jurisdiction where enrolled [Yes or No] (If no, Where); Ward [Yes or No]; Allotment, Annuity, and Identification Numbers.

1314; De Ye Te; m; 40 (1892); F; m; Head; yes; yes; *(Blank)*
1315; Do Ye Te's Wife; f; 26 (1906); F; m; wife; yes; yes; 2909

1316; Wood; m; ?; F; s; Head; yes; yes; 2911

1317; Do Ye Te Hostine; m; 62 (1870); F; m; Head; yes; yes; 6305
1318; Do Ye Te Hostine's Wife; f; 48 (1884); F; m; wife; yes; yes; 6303
1319; Hostine Nez; m; ?; F; s; son; yes; yes; 6406
1320; Hostine Bega; m; 27 (1905); F; s; son; yes; yes; 6455
1321; Nellie; f; 25 (1907); F; s; dau; yes; yes; 6306
1322; Yazza Yazza; f; 21 (1911); F; s; dau; yes; yes; 6433
1323; Hoske Newood, Joe; m; 18 (1914); F; s; grnd-son; yes; yes; 4524
1324; Zah Gey, Nellie; f; 7 (1925); F; s; grnd-dau; yes; yes; 6304
1325; Zennie Soice; f; 4 (1928); F; s; grnd-dau; yes; yes; 6307
1326; Socie Clah, Yellow Hair; m; 6 (1926); F; s; grnd-son; yes; yes; 6302

1327; Elizibel; f; 23 (1909); F; w; Head; yes; yes; 2492
1328; Ah Kee; m; 4 (1928); F; s; son; yes; yes; 2493

1329; Eschee; m; 67 (1865); F; m; Head; yes; yes; 6401
1330; Ah He De Bah; f; 53 (1879); F; m; wife; yes; yes; *(Blank)*
1331; Eschee's Son; m; 31 (1901); F; s; son; yes; yes; *(Blank)*
1332; Waya, Emerson; m; 18 (1914); F; s; grnd-son; yes; yes; 6014
1333; Atah Ate De; f; 12 (1920); F; s; grnd-dau; yes; yes; 6403
1334; De Zah he; m; 8 (1924); F; s; grnd-son; yes; yes; 6404
1335; Mabel; f; 30 (1902); F; s; dau; yes; yes; *(Blank)*
1336; Dan #3; f; 7 (1925); F; s; dau; yes; yes; *(Blank)*
1337; Dan #4; f; 8 (1924); F; s; dau; yes; yes; *(Blank)*
1338; Ah Way; m; 4 (1928); F; s; son; yes; yes; *(Blank)*

1339; Esquela Bega #8; m; 23 (1909); F; s; Head; yes; yes; 6948
1340; Smith, Grace; f; 16 (1916); F; s; ?; yes; yes; *(Blank)*
1341; Ash Ke De Bah; f; 16 (1916); F; s; sis; yes; yes; *(Blank)*
1342; Asdanab Bah, Hilda; f; 11 (1921); f; s; sis; yes; yes; *(Blank)*
1343; Deswood Hoskie; m; 9 (1923); F; s; bro; yes; yes; 6344
1344; Yana Wood; m; 7 (1925); F; s; bro; yes; yes; 6345

1345; Esta Na; m; 27 (1905); F; w; Head; yes; yes; *(Blank)*
1346; Esta; f; 9 (1923); F; s; dau; yes; yes; *(Blank)*
1347; Kahn; f; 7 (1925); F; s; dau; yes; yes; *(Blank)*
1348; Schan; m; 5 (1927); F; s; son; yes; yes; 3928

1349; Etoity Yazza; m; 41 (1891); F; m; Head; yes; yes; 2865
1350; Etoity Yazza Bay Aszan; f; 31 (1901); F; m; wife; yes; yes; 2866

NAVAJO INDIAN CENSUS, (As of April 1, 1932)
KEY: Census Number; Name; Sex; Age at Last Birthday; Tribe (Navajo, unless otherwise stated); Degree of Blood; Marital Status; Relationship to Head of Family; At Jurisdiction where enrolled [Yes or No] (If no, Where); Ward [Yes or No]; Allotment, Annuity, and Identification Numbers.

1351; Badona, Ray; m; 15 (1917); F; s; son; yes; yes; 2867
1352; Ray's Brother; m; 13 (1919); F; s; son; yes; yes; 2868
1353; Guy Socie; m; 9 (1923); F; s; son; yes; yes; 2869
1354; Chee Barn; m; 7 (1925); F; s; son; yes; yes; 2870
1355; Ahade; f; 6 (1926); F; s; dau; yes; yes; 2871
1356; Hoskie; m; 4 (1928); F; s; son; yes; yes; 2872
1357; Hosteen Nez Day Aszan; f; 35 (1897); F; s; wife #2; yes; yes; 2873
1358; Kee Socie; m; 13 (1919); F; s; son; yes; yes; 2874
1359; Guy Aye Soi; m; 13 (1919); F; s; son; yes; yes; 2875
1360; Ken Yazza; m; 7 (1925); F; s; dau[sic]; yes; yes; 2876
1361; Gee; m; 4 (1928); F; s; son; yes; yes; 2877

1362; Etsidy; m; ?; F; m; Head; yes; yes; 6377
1363; Etsidy's Wife; f; 74 (1858); f; m; wife; yes; yes; 6368
1364; Etsidy's Daughter; f; 38 (1894); F; s; dau; yes; yes; 6374
1365; Bahhe; m; 13 (1928); F; s; grnd-son; yes; yes; 6376
1366; Bitsoni; m; 22 (1910); F; s; son; yes; yes; 6373

1367; Etsidy Bega; m; 53 (1879); F; m; Head; yes; yes; 5716
1368; Slah Bitsi; f; 52 (1880); F; m; wife; yes; yes; 5643
1369; Aszan Socie; f; 29 (1903); F; s; dau; yes; yes; 5644
1370; Na; m; 27 (1905); F; s; son; yes; yes; 5679
1371; Schonnie; f; 25 (1907); F; s; dau; yes; yes; 5645
1372; Smith, Tilman; m; 20 (1912); F; s; son; yes; yes; 5717
1373; Smith, Sally; f; 17 (1915); F; s; dau; yes; yes; 5646
1374; Smith, Denna; m; 14 (1918); F; s; son; yes; yes; 5718
1375; Nah Zien; m; 12 (1920); F; s; son; yes; yes; 5719
1376; Cho Ho; m; 9 (1923); F; s; son; yes; yes; 5647
1377; Ah Ade Chone; f; 4 (1928); F; s; dau; yes; yes; 5648

1378; Etsitty Son; m; 61 (1871); F; m; Head; yes; yes; 6489
1379; Etsitty's Son's Wife; f; 42 (1890); F; m; wife; yes; yes; 6399
1380; Sonne; f; 16 (1916); F; s; dau; yes; yes; 6398
1381; Bahhe; f; 18 (1914); F; s; dau; yes; yes; 5812
1382; Yazza Bah; f; 10 (1922); F; s; dau; yes; yes; 4182
1383; Cle See; m; 6 (1926); F; s; son; yes; yes; 6011
1384; Ah He; f; 5 (1927); F; s; dau; yes; yes; 6397

1385; Fhe Wah He; m; 62 (?); F; w; Head; yes; yes; 1336

1386; Frank; m; ?; F; m; Head; yes; yes; 1110
1387; Zahns Soi; f; 21 (1911); F; m; wife; yes; yes; 11
1388; May; f; 3 (1929); F; s; dau; yes; yes; 1167

NAVAJO INDIAN CENSUS, (As of April 1, 1932)
KEY: Census Number; Name; Sex; Age at Last Birthday; Tribe (Navajo, unless otherwise stated); Degree of Blood; Marital Status; Relationship to Head of Family; At Jurisdiction where enrolled [Yes or No] (If no, Where); Ward [Yes or No]; Allotment, Annuity, and Identification Numbers.

1389; Frank; m; 34 (1898); F; m; Head; yes; yes; 145
1390; Ah Soi Ne Gees Bah; f; 30 (1902); F; m; wife; yes; yes; 155
1391; Nah Gle Nes Bah; f; 8 (1924); F; s; dau; yes; yes; 125
1392; Frank, Milton; m; 4 (1928); F; s; son; yes; yes; 141
1393; Ha Cha Yazze; m; 3 (1929); F; s; son; yes; yes; *(Blank)*
1394; Hos Che Yazzie; m; 3 (1929); F; s; son; yes; yes; 958

1395; Frank; m; 23 (1909); F; s; Head; yes; yes; 1360
1396; Jack; m; 10 (1922); F; s; bro; yes; yes; 848
1397; Ye Ha Bah; f; 9 (1923); F; s; sis; yes; yes; 849
1398; Si He; m; ?; F; s; ?; yes; yes; *(Blank)*

1399; Frank, Wife of Charley; f; 48 (1884); F; w; Head; yes; yes; 596
1400; Frank, Tom; m; 25 (1907); F; s; son; yes; yes; 407
1401; Frank, Jack; m; 18 (1914); F; s; son; yes; yes; 597

1402; Gemmie, Old Hosteen; m; 72 (1860); F; w; Head; yes; yes; 1687

1403; Gana Bay Aszan, Old Hosteen; f; ?; F; w; Head; yes; yes; 334
1404; Gene; m; 19 (1923); F; s; son; yes; yes; 1690
1405; Mary; f; 18 (1914); F; s; dau; yes; yes; 319
1406; Gana, Jack; m; 16 (1916); F; s; son; yes; yes; 1692
1407; No Tah; m; 10 (1922); F; s; son; yes; yes; 320
1408; Emory; m; 9 (1923); F; s; son; yes; yes; 1693
1409; Cay Cans Bah; f; 9 (1923); F; s; dau; yes; yes; 321
1410; Ye Cahs; m; 4 (1928); F; s; son; yes; yes; 335

1411; Gee, Claire; m; 40 (1892); F; m; Head; yes; yes; 369
1412; Bis Kee; m; 19 (1913); F; s; son; yes; yes; 371
1413; Irene; f; 17 (1915); F; s; dau; yes; yes; 1127
1414; Aszan Be Toe Ne; f; 38 (1894); F; m; wife; yes; yes; 374
1415; Bessie; f; 20 (1912); F; s; dau; yes; 960
1416; Lucy; f; 9 (1923); F; s; dau; yes; yes; 961
1417; Tuce; m; 10 (1922); F; s; son; yes; yes; 375
1418; Dah Na Bah; f; 8 (1924); F; s; dau; yes; yes; 376
1419; Da Be Bah; f; 6 (1926); F; s; dau; yes; yes; 377

1420; Gee, Guy; m; 46 (1886); F; m; Head; yes; yes; 317
1421; Hosteen Gana Bitse #2; f; 31 (1901); F; m; wife; yes; yes; 318

1422; Gene Benally Hosteen; m; 27 (1905); F; m; Head; yes; yes; 3808
1423; Athsecth Benna; f; 27 (1905); F; m; wife; yes; yes; 3809
1424; Athsecth; f; 3 (1929); F; s; dau; yes; yes; 3810

NAVAJO INDIAN CENSUS, (As of April 1, 1932)

KEY: Census Number; Name; Sex; Age at Last Birthday; Tribe (Navajo, unless otherwise stated); Degree of Blood; Marital Status; Relationship to Head of Family; At Jurisdiction where enrolled [Yes or No] (If no, Where); Ward [Yes or No]; Allotment, Annuity, and Identification Numbers.

1425; Gene Gega, Hosteen; m; 33 (1899); F; m; Head; yes; yes; *(Blank)*
1426; Zah Bema; f; 33 (1899); F; m; wife; yes; yes; 204
*1426; Smith, Henry; m; 12 (1920); F; s; son; no; Ft. Apache School, P.O. Ft. Apache, Apache Co, AZ; yes; *(Blank)* *(*NOTE: Number given twice)*

1427; Gene Ne No. Hosteen; m; 43 (1889); F; m; Head; yes; yes; 520
1428; Sa Ei Bitse; f; 39 (1893); F; m; wife; yes; yes; 521
1429; Bah; f; 10 (1922); F; s; dau; yes; yes; *(Blank)*
1430; Gene Be Nelly, Eddie; m; 18 (1914); F; s; son; no; Ft. Apache School, P.O. Ft. Apache, Apache Co, AZ; yes; 978
1431; Morris; m; 19 (1913); F; s; son; no; Truxton Canyon, P.O. Valentine, AZ; yes; 979

1432; George, m; 32 (1900); F; m; Head; yes; yes; 2931
1433; Aszan, Pearl; f; 30 (1902); F; m; wife; yes; yes; 2932
1434; Hoskie Ne Tee; m; 2 (1930); F; s; son; yes; yes; *(Blank)*

1435; George, John; m; 24 (1908); F; m; Head; yes; yes; 180
1436; Aszan Guy; f; 35 (1897); F; m; wife; yes; yes; 293
1437; Ah Na Bah; f; 14 (1918); F; m; dau; yes; yes; 294
1438; Lily; f; 10 (1922); F; s; dau; yes; yes; 42
1439; Che Ha Bah; f; 7 (1925); F; s; dau; yes; yes; 108

(NOTE: Numbered as is on original.)

2737; Socie Zah Nez; m; 77 (1855); F; w; Head; yes; yes; 3883

2738; Soi, Aszan; f; 35 (1897); F; s; Head; yes; yes; 737
2739; Ah Kee; m; 13 (1919); F; s; son; yes; yes; 78
2740; Woody; m; 11 (1921); F; s; son; yes; yes; 1314
2741; Yazze; m; 8 (1924); F; s; son; yes; yes; 80
2742; Bah Des Wood; f; 7 (1925); F; s; dau; yes; yes; 738
2743; Gli Ha Bah; f; 5 (1927); F; s; dau; yes; yes; 739

2744; Soi, Aszan; f; 81 (1851); F; w; Head; yes; yes; 5630
2745; Soi Aszan Bega; f; 44 (1888); F; w; dau; yes; yes; 5631
2746; Datenany, Susie; f; 20 (1912); F; s; grnd-dau; yes; yes; 5632
2747; Datenany, Violet; f; 18 (1914); F; s; grnd-dau; yes; yes; 5715
2748; Mozzie; f; 11 (1921); F; grnd-dau; yes; yes; *(Blank)*
2749; Si He; m; 8 (1924); F; s; grnd-son; yes; yes; 5638
2750; Datenany, Norton; m; 15 (1917); F; s; grnd-son; yes; yes; *(Blank)*
2751; Nee He; f; 24 (1908); F; s; orphan; yes; yes; 5634
2752; Dena; m; 23 (1909); F; s; ?; yes; yes; 5722
2753; Tommy; m; 21 (1911); F; s; ?; yes; yes; 5721

NAVAJO INDIAN CENSUS, (As of April 1, 1932)

KEY: Census Number; Name; Sex; Age at Last Birthday; Tribe (Navajo, unless otherwise stated); Degree of Blood; Marital Status; Relationship to Head of Family; At Jurisdiction where enrolled [Yes or No] (If no, Where); Ward [Yes or No]; Allotment, Annuity, and Identification Numbers.

2754; Soi Ba Doni, Hosteen; m; 38 (1894); F; m; Head; yes; yes; 559
2755; Hosteen Soi Bitsie; f; 36 (1897); F; m; wife; yes; yes; 560
2756; White, Fanny; f; 15 (1917); F; s; dau; no; Ft. Apache, P.O. Ft. Apache, Apache Co, AZ; yes; *(Blank)*
2757; Toli; f; 13 (1919); F; s; dau; yes; yes; 564
2758; Sihe; m; 11 (1921); F; s; son; yes; yes; 565
2759; Na Nes Bah; f; 9 (1923); F; s; dau; yes; yes; *(Blank)*
2760; Guy Yazze; f; 7 (1925); F; s; dau; yes; yes; 566
2761; Clay Chi Be Ahs Dog Bitten; m; 6 (1926); F; s; son; yes; yes; 567
2762; Yah Yazze; m; 5 (1927); F; s; son; yes; yes; 568

2763; Soi, Hosteen; m; 83 (1849); F; m; Head; yes; yes; 2860
2764; Soi, Hosteen, Wife #1; f; 61 (1871); F; m; wife; yes; yes; 2861
2765; Soi, Hosteen, Wife #2; f; 42 (1890); F; m; wife; yes; yes; 2862
2766; Denna Bahhe; m; 37 (1895); F; s; son; yes; yes; 2863
2767; Begay, Mark; m; 23 (1909); F; s; son; yes; yes; 2456
2768; Zan; f; 16 (1916); F; s; dau; yes; yes; 2854

2769; Soi, Hosteen; m; 37 (1895); F; m; Head; yes; yes; *(Blank)*
2770; Aszan Soi; f; 36 (1896); F; m; wife; yes; yes; *(Blank)*
2771; Kee Chee; m; 9 (1923); F; s; son; yes; yes; *(Blank)*

(NOTE: Numbered as is on original.)

2778; Soi Bega Badoni, Hosteen; m; 26 (1906); F; m; Head; yes; yes; 4259
2779; Zoni Soi; f; 21 (1911); F; m; wife; yes; yes; 4260
2780; Kee Yazza; m; 3 (1929); F; s; son; yes; yes; 4261
2781; Chans Na Bah; f; 26 (1906); F; m; wife; yes; yes; 4262
2782; Kee Chee; m; 6 (1926); F; s; son; yes; yes; 4263
2783; Ah Tade Chee; m; 5 (1927); F; s; son; yes; yes; 4264

2784; Soi Bega, Hosteen; m; 37 (1895); F; m; Head; yes; yes; 4250
2785; Aszan Soi Benna; f; 42 (1890); F; m; wife; yes; yes; 4251
2786; Soi Begay, Lorene; f; 19 (1913); F; s; dau; yes; yes; 4252
2781; Yazza; f; 17 (1915); F; s; dau; yes; yes; 4485
2782; Soi Begay, Eugene; m; 14 (1918); F; s; son; yes; yes; 4486
2783; Cho Li; f; 12 (1920); F; s; dau; yes; yes; 4487
2784; Nah Cli; f; 9 (1923); F; s; dau; yes; yes; 4253
2785; Ah Tade Yazza; F; 7 (1925); F; s; dau; yes; yes; 4254
2786; A Lah Socie; m; 21 (1911); F; s; nephew; yes; yes; 4255
2787; Aszan Yo In Title; f; 57 (1875); F; m; wife; yes; yes; 4256
2788; Raymond; m; 2 (1930); F; s; son; yes; yes; 4478

2789; Soi, Hosteen; m; 48 (1884); F; w; Head; yes; yes; 4234

NAVAJO INDIAN CENSUS, (As of April 1, 1932)
KEY: Census Number; Name; Sex; Age at Last Birthday; Tribe (Navajo, unless otherwise stated); Degree of Blood; Marital Status; Relationship to Head of Family; At Jurisdiction where enrolled [Yes or No] (If no, Where); Ward [Yes or No]; Allotment, Annuity, and Identification Numbers.

2790; Soi, Hosteen; m; 83 (1849); F; m; Head; yes; yes; 4238
2791; Aszan Zinny; f; 60 (1872); F; m; wife; yes; yes; 4237
2792; Ah Tade Yazza; f; 24 (1908); F; s; dau; yes; yes; 4246
2793; Ah Ba Bah; f; 16 (1916); F; s; dau; yes; yes; *(Blank)*

2794; Sone, Hosteen; m; 47 (1885); F; m; Head; yes; yes; 5807
2795; Zed Dah So Ahloni Bitsi; f; 27 (1905); F; m; wife; yes; yes; 5808
2796; Aszan Chee; f; 12 (1920); F; s; dau; yes; yes; 5805
2797; Bah Ye De; f; 5 (1927); F; s; dau; yes; yes; 5809

2798; Soui, Hosteen; m; 30 (1902); F; m; Head; yes; yes; 1490
2799; Yazza, Nettie; f; 18 (1914); F; m; wife; yes; yes; 1491
2800; Aszan Nez; f; 3 (1929); F; s; dau; yes; yes; 1640

2801; Tah Bah; m; 41 (1891); F; m; Head; yes; yes; 3764
2802; Tah Bahhe; f; 40 (1892); F; m; wife; yes; yes; 3611
2803; Zannie; f; 16 (1916); F; s; dau; yes; yes; 5326
2804; Ha Ha Gleen; m; 8 (1924); F; s; son; yes; yes; 3022

2805; Tah Bahhe; m; ?; F; m; Head; yes; yes; 1466
2806; Na Glee Ne Bah; f; ?; F; m; wife; yes; yes; 1459
2807; Peck, Enoch; m; 23 (1909); F; s; son; yes; yes; 1460

2808; T Bah He, Aszan; f; 53 (1879); F; w; Head; yes; yes; 178
2809; Hoskie De Wood, Otho; m; 16 (1916); F; s; son; yes; yes; 179

2810; Ta Bah He Bega; m; 27 (1805); F; w; Head; yes; yes; 483
2811; Bahhe; f; 5 (1927); F; s; dau; yes; yes; 485
2812; Kan Bahhe; f; 5 (1927); F; s; dau; yes; yes; 3318
2813; Hoska Nae Wood; m; 6 (1926); F; s; son; yes; yes; 3317
2814; Kan Soie; f; 2 91930); F; s; dau; yes; yes; 3319

2815; Ta Bah He Soue; m; 48 (1884); F; m; Head; yes; yes; 344
2816; Ta Bah He Soue's Wife; f; 48 (1884); F; m; wife; yes; yes; 348

2817; Tah Bah He Socie Bega; m; 35 (1897); F; m; Head; yes; yes; 525
2818; Denet Bahhe Bema; f; 28 (1904); F; m; wife; yes; yes; 468
2819; Denet Bahhe; m; 5 (1927); F; s; son; yes; yes; 469
2820; Ada Kai; f; 3 (1929); F; s; dau; yes; yes; 999

2821; Ta Chee Ne, Aszan; m; 57 (1875); F; w; Head; yes; yes; 471

2822; Ta Chee Ne, Aszan; f; 78 (1854); F; w; Head; yes; yes; *(Blank)*

43

NAVAJO INDIAN CENSUS, (As of April 1, 1932)

KEY: Census Number; Name; Sex; Age at Last Birthday; Tribe (Navajo, unless otherwise stated); Degree of Blood; Marital Status; Relationship to Head of Family; At Jurisdiction where enrolled [Yes or No] (If no, Where); Ward [Yes or No]; Allotment, Annuity, and Identification Numbers.

2823; Tah Dis Bah; f; ?; F; w; Head; yes; yes; 54
2824; Tah; m; 10 (1922); F; s; son; yes; yes; 52
2825; Al Ka They Bah; f; 17 (1915); F; s; dau; yes; yes; 1142

2826; Tah Na Ne Guy; m; 41 (1891); F; m; Head; yes; yes; *(Blank)*
2827; Ken; f; 30 (1902); F; m; wife; yes; yes; *(Blank)*

2828; Tah Ne Zahne Socie; m; 33 (1899); F; w; Head; yes; yes; 4258

2829; Ta Ne Zah; m; 23 (1909); F; m; Head; yes; yes; 4495
2830; Bahhe; f; 18 (1914); F; m; wife; yes; yes; 3691
2831; Johnnie; m; 6 (1926); F; s; son; yes; yes; 3690
2832; Ah Ade; f; 4 (1928); F; s; dau; yes; yes; 3687
2833; Ad Swe See Hoskie; m; 3 (1929); F; s; son; yes; yes; *(Blank)*
2834; Yazze Yie Hosteen Bela; f; 23 (1909); F; m; wife; yes; yes; 3688

2835; Tat Na Zahne Socie; m; 30 (1902); F; m; Head; yes; yes; *(Blank)*
2836; Zahns Goy; f; 29 (1903); F; m; wife; yes; yes; *(Blank)*
2837; Hoskie Chee He; m; 5 (1927); F; s; son; yes; yes; *(Blank)*
2838; Ah Ade Chee He; f; 4 (1928); F; s; dau; yes; yes; *(Blank)*
2839; White Man, Albert; m; 25 (1907); F; s; son; yes; yes; 3947

2840; Ta Ye Soi He, John Scott; m; 27 (1905); F; m; Head; yes; yes; 1416
2841; Ye Ta Ne Bah; f; 25 (1907); F; m; wife; yes; yes; 1417
2842; Ah Hes De Bah; f; 6 (1926); F; s; dau; yes; yes; 1418
2843; Na Dach Na De Ya; m; 4 (1928); F; s; son; yes; yes; 1419
2844; Chee Zin Bin Ne; m; 4 (1928); F; s; son; yes; yes; 4419
2845; Hoskie Asocie; m; 3 (1929); F; s; son; yes; yes; 4426

2846; Thise Aszan; f; 61 (1871); F; w; Head; yes; yes; 6354
2847; Ash Socie Bah, Priscilla; f; 16 (1916); F; s; grnd-dau; yes; yes; 6353

2848; Ta Ni Zane Yazza; m; 36 (1896); F; m; Head; yes; yes; *(Blank)*
2849; Cis See; f; 24 (1908); F; m; wife; yes; yes; 1520
2850; Aday Yazza; f; 16 (1916); F; s; dau; yes; yes; 1649
2851; Knox; m; 13 (1919); F; s; son; yes; yes; *(Blank)*
2852; Denet Chee; m; 11 (1921); F; s; son; yes; yes; *(Blank)*
2853; Aday Chee; f; 6 (1926); F; s; dau; yes; yes; 1650
2854; Elsie; f; ?; F; s; sis; yes; yes; *(Blank)*

2855; Tat Chee Ne; m; 62 (1870); F; m; Head; yes; yes; 3648
2856; Nez Aszan; f; 58 (1874); F; m; wife; yes; yes; 3654
2857; Aszan Yazza; f; 4 (1928); F; s; dau; yes; yes; 4458
2858; Aszan Socie; f; 3 (1929); F; s; dau; yes; yes; 4456

NAVAJO INDIAN CENSUS, (As of April 1, 1932)
KEY: Census Number; Name; Sex; Age at Last Birthday; Tribe (Navajo, unless otherwise stated); Degree of Blood; Marital Status; Relationship to Head of Family; At Jurisdiction where enrolled [Yes or No] (If no, Where); Ward [Yes or No]; Allotment, Annuity, and Identification Numbers.

2859; Thick Woman; f; 31 (1901); F; s[sic]; wife #2; yes; yes; *(Blank)*
2860; Ah Ehe Hoskie; m; 5 (1927); F; s; son; yes; yes; 3655

2861; Tee Ne; m; ?; F; m; Head; yes; yes; 987
2862; Te Ne's Wife; f; 43 (1889); F; m; wife; yes; yes; 988
2863; Albert; m; 21 (1911); f; s; son; yes; yes; 989
2864; Kee; m; 19 (1913); F; s; son; no; Ft. Apache School, P.O. Ft. Apache, Apache Co, AZ; 990
2865; Kee Yazze; m; 15 (1917); F; s; son; yes; yes; 991
2866; Bah; f; 6 (1926); F; s; dau; yes; yes; 992

2867; To Ad Lena, Aszan; f; 65 (1867); F; w; Head; yes; yes; 540

2868; Toe Ah Hanie; m; 73 (1859); F; m; Head; yes; yes; 2933
2869; Boy Aszan; f; 61 (1981); F; m; wife; yes; yes; 2899

2870; To Ba Honani Begay; m; ?; F; m; Head; yes; yes; *(Blank)*
2871; Zahn Guy; f; 20 (1912); F; m; wife; yes; yes; 1578

2872; To De Chenah Denah; m; 32 (1900); F; m; Head; yes; yes; 6465
2873; Bah Keane; f; 28 (1904); F; m; wife; yes; yes; 6446
2874; Bah Gee; f; 10 (1922); F; s; dau; yes; yes; 4149
2875; Socie Dennet; m; 12 (1920); F; s; son; yes; yes; *(Blank)*

2876; To De Chene; m; 43 (1889); F; m; Head; yes; yes; 6497
2877; Ahs Nah Bah; f; 33 (1899); F; m; wife; yes; yes; 6343
2878; Sophia; f; 39 (1893); F; s; ?; yes; yes; 4511
2879; Cardy Bah; f; 5 (1927); F; s; grnd-dau; yes; yes; *(Blank)*
2880; Ah Ta De Bah; f; 7 (1925); F; s; grnd-dau; yes; yes; 6346
2881; Glenn; f; 23 (1909); F; s; dau; yes; yes; 6341
2882; Hosk Yel He Wad; m; 4 (1928); F; s; son; yes; yes; 4513

2883; To La Son; ?; 67 (1865); F; w; Head; yes; yes; 5826
2884; Zan Se He; f; 15 (1917); F; s; dau; yes; yes; 5817
2885; Woode; m; 11 (1921); F; s; son; yes; yes; 5828
2886; Za He; m; 33 (1899); F; s; son; yes; yes; 5829
2887; Chee, Waldine*; f; 13 (1919); F; s; dau; yes; yes; 5908
2888; Aszan Choola; f; 7 (1925); F; s; dau; yes; yes; 5909
2889; Tso Die; f; 5 (1927); F; s; dau; yes; yes; 5910
2890; Yazza; m; 4 (1928); F; s; son; yes; yes; 5911

(*NOTE: Name difficult to read)

2891; Toe Ah Honni Begay; m; 43 (1889); F; m; Head; yes; yes; 2445
2892; Toe Ah Honni Begay's Wife; f; 43 (1889); F; m; wife; yes; yes; 2446

NAVAJO INDIAN CENSUS, (As of April 1, 1932)

KEY: Census Number; Name; Sex; Age at Last Birthday; Tribe (Navajo, unless otherwise stated); Degree of Blood; Marital Status; Relationship to Head of Family; At Jurisdiction where enrolled [Yes or No] (If no, Where); Ward [Yes or No]; Allotment, Annuity, and Identification Numbers.

2893; Glenn; f; 16 (1916); F; s; dau; yes; yes; 2447
2894; Edna; f; 14 (1918); F; s; dau; yes; yes; 2900
2895; Lola; f; 13 (1919); F; s; dau; yes; yes; 2901
2896; Yah De Wood; m; 11 (1921); F; s; son; yes; yes; 2448
2897; Yah Ne Bah; f; 10 (1922); F; s; dau; yes; yes; 2449
2898; Tanie Sa Ne Yazza; m; 4 (1928); F; s; son; yes; yes; 2450

2899; Toe Cle Chene, Hosteen; m; ?; F; w; Head; yes; yes; *(Blank)*
2900; Dick; m; 26 (1906); F; s; son; yes; yes; 1358

2901; Toe De Chee, Aszan; m; 75 (1857); F; m; Head; yes; yes; 3004
2902; Julia; f; 37 (1896); F; m; wife; yes; yes; *(Blank)*
2903; Yah De Bah; f; 23 (1909); F; s; dau; yes; yes; 3006
2904; Ah Ada Soi; f; 4 (19280; F; s; grnd-dau; yes; yes; 3004
2905; Si Chee; m; 17 (1915); F; s; grnd-son; yes; yes; 3363
2906; Toli; f; 19 (1913); F; s; grnd-dau; yes; yes; 3008

2907; Toe De Chene. Aszan; f; 35 (1897); F; w; Head; yes; yes; 432
2908; Clah; m; 23 (1907); f; s; bro; yes; yes; 939

2909; Toe De Chenne; m; ?; F; w; Head; yes; yes; *(Blank)*
2910; Nelson, May; f; 19 (1913); F; s; dau; yes; yes; 1499

2911; Toe De Cohns, Hosteen; m; 76 (1856); F; m; Head; yes; yes; 321
2912; Aszan Yazze; f; 48 (1884); F; m; wife; yes; yes; 208
2913; He Nic Aye, Benjamin; m; 20 (1912); F; s; son; yes; yes; *(Blank)*
2914; Bahhe; m; 7 (1925); F; s; son; yes; yes; 209

2915; Toedee Cohns Badoni; m; ?; F; m; Head; yes; yes; 241
2916; Toli Bema; f; 32 (1900); F; m; wife; yes; yes; 242
2917; Toli; m; 13 (1919); F; s; son; no; Leupp School, P.O. Leupp, Coconino Co, AZ; yes; *(Blank)*
2918; Ah Ade Chee; f; 10 (1922); F; s; dau; yes; yes; 243
2919; Chee Ne; m; 7 (1925); F; s; son; yes; yes; 244
2920; Soi; m; 5 (1927); F; s; son; yes; yes; 245
2921; Guy; f; 4 (1928); F; s; son; yes; yes; 1162

2922; Toe Honam; m; 57 (1875); F; m; Head; yes; yes; *(Blank)*
2923; Aszan; f; 44 (1888); F; m; wife; yes; yes; 5767
2924; Salah Bitsi Goody; m; 20 (1912); F; s; son; yes; yes; 5768
2925; She; f; 18 (1914); F; s; dau; yes; yes; 5769
2926; Sam; m; 17 (1915); F; s; son; yes; yes; 5770
2927; Jinney Toe Honani; f; 14 (1918); F; s; dau; yes; yes; 5771
2928; Joel; f; 12 (1920); F; s; dau; yes; yes; 5772

NAVAJO INDIAN CENSUS, (As of April 1, 1932)
KEY: Census Number; Name; Sex; Age at Last Birthday; Tribe (Navajo, unless otherwise stated); Degree of Blood; Marital Status; Relationship to Head of Family; At Jurisdiction where enrolled [Yes or No] (If no, Where); Ward [Yes or No]; Allotment, Annuity, and Identification Numbers.

2929; Bahhe; f; 6 (1926); f; s; dau; yes; yes; 5773
2930; Nas Cott; f; 4 (1928); F; s; dau; yes; yes; 5774

2931; Toe Honani Bay Aszan; f; 66 (1866); F; w; Head; yes; yes; 3372
2932; Etsidy; m; 43 (1889); F; s; son; yes; yes; 1429

2933; Toe Honani Bitse; m; 33 (1899); F; w; Head; yes; yes; 2912
2934; Laura; f; 18 (1914); F; s; dau; yes; yes; 2420
2935; Da Kai; f; 3 (1929); F; s; dau; yes; yes; 2429

2936; Toe Honani Hoskie; m; ?; F; m; Head; yes; yes; 3355
2937; Zahns Guy; f; 37 (1895); F; m; wife; yes; yes; 3556
2938; Chee; m; 11 (1921); F; s; son; yes; yes; *(Blank)*
2939; Kee; m; 5 (1927); F; s; son; yes; yes; 2967
2940; Tah Nezzie Soise; m; 2 (1930); F; s; son; yes; yes; *(Blank)*

2941; Toe Soi Ne Socie; m; ?; F; m; Head; yes; yes; 196
2942; Toe Soi Ne Socie's Wife; f; 30 (1902); F; m; wife; yes; yes; 197
2943; Wah De Bah; f; 8 (1924); F; s; dau; yes; yes; 109

2944; Tom; m; 40 (1892); F; m; Head; yes; yes; 3766
2945; Aszan Socie Benna; f; 23 (1909); F; m; wife; yes; yes; 3635
2946; Aszan Socie; f; 5 (1927); F; s; dau; yes; yes; 3636
2947; Donald; m; 3 (1929); F; s; son; yes; yes; 3637

2948; Tom Joe; m; 31 (1901); F; m; Head; yes; yes; 1430
2949; Hoskie Soi Bena; f; 31 (1901); F; m; wife; yes; yes; 1431
2950; Hoskie Soi; m; 7 (1925); F; s; son; yes; yes; 1432
2951; Hoskie Tas Wood; m; 4 (1928); F; s; son; yes; yes; 1433
2952; Ada Soice; f; 4 (1928); F; s; dau; yes; yes; 3375
2953; Hoskie Tahe; m; 2 (1930); F; s; son; yes; yes; 3376

2954; Toney; m; 68 (1864); F; m; Head; yes; yes; 310
2955; Bay Aszan Toney; f; 63 (1869); F; m; wife; yes; yes; 312
2956; Ah Tade Yazza; f; 5 (1927); F; s; dau; yes; yes; 311

2957; Toode Cheney; f; 68 (1964); F; w; Head; yes; yes; 6444
2958; Has Bah; f; 43 (1889); F; s; dau; yes; yes; 6445

2959; Ugashe; m; 28 (1904); F; w; Head; yes; yes; 4401
2960; Zonnie; f; 28 (1904); F; s; dau; yes; yes; 4402
2961; Kee Yazza; m; 12 (1920); F; s; son; yes; yes; 4161
2962; Jina Bah; f; 3 (1929); f; s; dau; yes; yes; 4296
2963; Si Hes Bah; f; 3 (1929); F; s; dau; yes; yes; 4221

NAVAJO INDIAN CENSUS, (As of April 1, 1932)
KEY: Census Number; Name; Sex; Age at Last Birthday; Tribe (Navajo, unless otherwise stated); Degree of Blood; Marital Status; Relationship to Head of Family; At Jurisdiction where enrolled [Yes or No] (If no, Where); Ward [Yes or No]; Allotment, Annuity, and Identification Numbers.

2964; Hoskie Bahhe; m; 11 (1921); F; s; grnd-son; yes; yes; 4297

2965; Ush Nes Nezzie, Aszan; f; 42 (1890); F; w; Head; yes; yes; 3799
2966; This He Kee; m; 20 (1912); F; s; son; yes; yes; *(Blank)*
2967; Sonnie Hosteen Yazzie; m; 18 (1914); F; s; son; yes; yes; *(Blank)*
2968; Yazzie De Hah Ya; m; 5 (1927); F; s; son; yes; yes; 3800

2969; Utan Hoskie; m; 40 (1892); F m; Head; yes; yes; 3840
2970; Nas Bah; f; 23 (1909); F; m; wife; yes; yes; 3837
2971; Tolea Kee; m; 7 (1925); F; s; grnd-son; yes; yes; 3927

2972; Walter, George; m; 33 (1899); F; m; Head; yes; yes; *(Blank)*
2973; Zanto, Bessie; f; 27 (1905); F; m; wife; yes; yes; *(Blank)*
2974; Dena, Fred; m; 33 (1899); F; s; bro-l; yes; yes; *(Blank)*

2975; Wartz; m; ?; F; m; Head; yes; yes; 3471

2976; Watson, Amy; f; 80 (1852); F; w; Head; yes; yes; 358
2977; Watson, Dan; m; 21 (1911); F; s; son; yes; yes; *(Blank)*
2978; Watson, Alfred; m; 14 (1918); F; s; son; yes; yes; *(Blank)*
2979; Watson, Don; m; ?; F; s; son; yes; yes; *(Blank)*

2980; Way, Aszan, Bayby Woman; f; 98 (1834); F; w; Head; yes; yes; 382
2981; Way She Ne Bahhe; f; 21 (1911); F; w; ead; yes; yes; 2495

2982; We Mozzir Dena Hosteen; m; 82 (1850); F; w; Head; yes; yes; 3929
2983; Nozzie Ad Ade; f; 9 (1923); F; s; grnd-dau; yes; yes; 3933
2984; Ad Ade Socie; m; 8 (1924); F; s; son; yes; yes; 3932

2985; Wesley; m; 48 (1884); F; m; Head; yes; yes; 5849
2986; Chisay Ja He Bitsi; f; 31 (1901); F; m; wife; yes; yes; 5850
2987; Chee Kee; m; 3 (1929); F; s; son; yes; yes; *(Blank)*
2988; Wesley, Charley; m; 18 (1914); F; s; son; yes; yes; 5851
2989; Chelly; f; 10 (1922); F; s; dau; yes; yes; 6067
2990; Zah Bahhe; f; 8 (1924); F; s; dau; yes; yes; 6098
2991; Yah Ne Bah; f; 6 (1926); F; s; dau; yes; yes; 5852
2992; Ye Ane Bah; f; 3 (1929); F; s; dau; yes; yes; 5853

2993; White Line Rock Man; m; ?; F; m; Head; yes; yes; *(Blank)*
2994; Ken He Bah; f; 47 (1995); F; m; wife; yes; yes; *(Blank)*
2995; Hoskie; m; 16 (1916); F; s; son; yes; yes; *(Blank)*
2996; Zahn; f; 14 (1918); f; s; dau; yes; yes; *(Blank)*
2997; Aszan Kai; f; 9 (1923); F; s; dau; yes; yes; *(Blank)*
2998; Be Ah Kee; m; 6 (1926); F; s; son; yes; yes; *(Blank)*

NAVAJO INDIAN CENSUS, (As of April 1, 1932)
KEY: Census Number; Name; Sex; Age at Last Birthday; Tribe (Navajo, unless otherwise stated); Degree of Blood; Marital Status; Relationship to Head of Family; At Jurisdiction where enrolled [Yes or No] (If no, Where); Ward [Yes or No]; Allotment, Annuity, and Identification Numbers.

2999; Kee Chee; m; 3 (1929); F; s; son; yes; yes; *(Blank)*

3000; White Man's Brother; m; 53 (1879); F; w; Head; yes; yes; *(Blank)*
3001; Se Se Zinna; f; 15 (1918)[sic]; F; s; dau; yes; yes; *(Blank)*
3002; Ze La Bah, Gordon; m; 12 (1920); F; s; son; yes; yes; 3931
3003; Fred; m; 10 (1922); F; s; son; yes; yes; 3935
3004; Aye Yaz; f; 4 (1928); F; s; dau; yes; yes; *(Blank)*

3005; Wide Foot; m; 74 (1858); F; m; Head; yes; yes; 3615
3006; Wide Foot's Wife; f; 38 (1894); F; m; wife; yes; yes; 3616
3007; Guy Zannie, Emma; f; 29 (1903); F; s; dau; yes; yes; 3617

3008; Wide Foot's Son; m; 23 (1909); F; m; Head; yes; yes; *(Blank)*
3009; Bahhe, Susie; f; 21 (1911); F; m; wife; yes; yes; 3509
3010; White Water's Son; m; 18 (1914); F; s; ?; yes; yes; 3904
3011; Tolea, June; f; 4 (1928); F; s; dau; yes; yes; 3508
3012; Socie; f; 19 (1913); F; s; ?; yes; yes; 3507
3013; Tolea; f; 17 (1915); F; s; ?; yes; yes; 3506
3014; Yazza, Grace; f; 15 (1917); F; s; ?; yes; yes; 3505
3015; Yith; f; 11 (1921); F; s; ?; yes; yes; 3504
3016; Yah; f; 9 (1823); F; s; ?; yes; yes; 3503
3017; Socie; m; 7 (1925); F; s; ?; yes; yes; *(Blank)*
3018; Yazza Hoskie; m; 4 (1928); F; s; son; yes; yes; 3502

3019; Wide Foot's Son; m; ?; F; m; Head; yes; yes; *(Blank)*
3020; Wide Foot's Son's Wife; f; 19 (1913); F; m; wife; yes; yes; *(Blank)*
3021; Susie; f; 14 (1918); F; s; dau; yes; yes; 3942
3022; Charlie; m; 13 (1919); F; s; son; yes; yes; 3430
3023; Ess Nezzie; m; 11 (1921); F; s; son; yes; yes; *(Blank)*
3024; Tolea; f; 6 (1926); F; s; dau; yes; yes; *(Blank)*
3025; White Man, Joe; m; 3 (1929); F; s; son; yes; yes; 3126
3026; White Man, Sam; m; 17 (1915); F; s; son; yes; yes; 3948
3027; Yazzie Ad Ade; f; 4 (1928); F; s; dau; yes; yes; 3724

3028; Willie, John; m; 53 (1879); F; m; Head; yes; yes; 3027
3029; Bay Aszan; f; 37 (1895); F; m; wife; yes; yes; 2934
3030; Jimmy; m; 19 91913); F; s; son; yes; yes; 2433
3031; William; m; 16 (1916); F; s; son; yes; yes; 2439
3032; Tah Ne Bah; f; 14 (1918); F; s; dau; yes; yes; *(Blank)*
3033; Kee Soi; m; 11 (1921); F; s; son; no; Leupp School, P.O. Leupp, Coconino Co, AZ; yes; 2437
3034; Kee; m; 9 (1923); F; s; son; yes; yes; 2438
3035; Kee Yazze; m; 6 (1926); F; s; son; yes; yes; 2935
3036; Hoskie Toli; m; 4 (1928); F; s; son; yes; yes; 2936

NAVAJO INDIAN CENSUS, (As of April 1, 1932)
KEY: Census Number; Name; Sex; Age at Last Birthday; Tribe (Navajo, unless otherwise stated); Degree of Blood; Marital Status; Relationship to Head of Family; At Jurisdiction where enrolled [Yes or No] (If no, Where); Ward [Yes or No]; Allotment, Annuity, and Identification Numbers.

3037; Yah Ne Bah; f; 9 (1923); F; s; dau; yes; yes; 2434
3038; Socie; m; 6 (1927); F; s; son; yes; yes; 4593
3039; Kee Toli; m; ?; F; s; son; yes; yes; *(Blank)*

3040; Willie, John; m; 33 (1899); F; m; Head; yes; yes; 2999
3041; Louise; f; 29 (1903); F; m; wife; yes; yes; 3000
3042; John, Jr; m; 7 (1925); F; s; son; yes; yes; *(Blank)*
3043; Willie, Fred; m; 3 (1929); F; s; son; yes; yes; *(Blank)*
3044; Willie, May; f; 5 (1927); F; s; dau; yes; yes; 3001

3045; Willie Begay; m; 44 (1888); F; m; Head; yes; yes; 3384
3046; Bah Ye Gee Bah; f; 28 (1904); f; m; wife; yes; yes; 1510
3047; Chee; f; 6 (1926); F; s; dau; yes; yes; 1511
3048; Bahhe; f; 5 (1927); F; s; dau; yes; yes; 1512
3049; Chee Ye Yazza; m; 3 (1929); F; s; son; yes; yes; 1648
3050; Kee Ne Chonie; m; 27 (1905); F; s; son; yes; yes; 1647
3051; Ruby; f; 17 (1915); F; s; dau; yes; yes; 1517
3052; Bahhe; m; 11 (1921); F; s; son; yes; yes; 1514
3053; Ah Hayne Bah; f; 9 (1923); F; s; dau; yes; yes; 1515
3054; Aszan Schene; f; 8 (1924); F; s; dau; yes; yes; 1516
3055; Hoskie Dah He Ya; m; 5 (1927); F; s; son; yes; yes; *(Blank)*
3056; Paul; m; 21 (1911); F; s; son; yes; yes; 1607

3057; Wilson, Joe; m; 26 (1906); F; m; Head; yes; yes; 4289
3058; Kan; f; 26 (1906); F; m; wife; yes; yes; 4290
3059; Denet Toli; m; 6 (1926); F; s; son; yes; yes; 4291

3060; Wilson, John; m; 31 (1901); F; s; Head; yes; yes; 1353

3061; Wilson, Woodrow; m; 64 (1878); F; m; Head; yes; yes; 590
3062; Benna, Edward; f; 46 (1886); F; m; wife; yes; yes; 591
3063; Edward, Archie; m; 24 (1908); F; s; son; yes; yes; 595
3064; Wilson, Archie; m; 19 (1913); F; s; son; yes; yes; 594
3065; Ne Zi Bah; f; 7 (1925); F; s; dau; yes; yes; 593
3066; Ne Ta Ye Tie; m; 2 (1930); F; s; son; yes; yes; 577

3067; Wilson Man; m; 44 (1988); F; m; Head; yes; yes; 3763
3068; Wilson Man's Wife; f; 29 (1903); F; m; wife; yes; yes; 3894
3069; Na Zeln; f; 19 (1922); F; s; dau; yes; yes; 3895
3070; Aszan Guy; f; 8 (1924); F; s; dau; yes; yes; 3896
3071; Bahhe; f; 6 (1926); F; s; dau; yes; yes; 3897
3072; Zahn Soi; f; 3 (1929); F; s; dau; yes; yes; 3898
3073; Aszan Socie; f; 4 (1892); F; m; wife; yes; yes; 3767
3074; Ah So Na De Bah; f; 8 (1924); F; s; dau; yes; yes; *(Blank)*

NAVAJO INDIAN CENSUS, (As of April 1, 1932)
KEY: Census Number; Name; Sex; Age at Last Birthday; Tribe (Navajo, unless otherwise stated); Degree of Blood; Marital Status; Relationship to Head of Family; At Jurisdiction where enrolled [Yes or No] (If no, Where); Ward [Yes or No]; Allotment, Annuity, and Identification Numbers.

3075; Zannie Tolea; f; 9 (1923); F; s; dau; yes; yes; 3768
3076; Hoskie Bahhe; m; 7 (1925); F; s; son; yes; yes; 3769
3077; Ad Etch Bahhe; m; 3 (1929); F; s; son; yes; yes; 3770

3078; Winker; m; ?; F; m; Head; yes; yes; 331
3079; Bah; f; 36 (1896); F; m; wife; yes; yes; 322
3080; Yeth Na Do Ne; m; 22 (1910); F; s; son; yes; yes; 1691
3081; Gay Ne Bah; f; 23 (1909); F; s; dau; yes; yes; 323
3082; Do Yazze; f; 8 (1924); F; s; dau; yes; yes; 324
3083; Bah Yazze; f; 7 (1925); F; s; dau; yes; yes; 325
3084; Ye Cat Da Su Ze; m; 5 (1927); F; s; son; yes; yes; 326
3085; Ye Ne No Da, Andrew; m; 16 (1916); F; s; son; yes; yes; 333
3086; Bahhe; m; 14 (19180; F; s; son; yes; yes; *(Blank)*
3087; Ya Na Bah; f; 12 (1920); F; s; dau; yes; yes; 332
3088; Ya Na Ne Bah; f; 38 (1894); F; s; dau; yes; yes; 328
3089; Yeth Ne Li Wood; m; 19 (1913); F; s; son; yes; yes; *(Blank)*
3090; Kirkton, Leo; m; 16 (1916); F; s; son; no; Ft. Apache School, P.O. Ft. Apache, Apache Co, AZ; yes; *(Blank)*
3091; Kirk, Charles; m; 16 (1916); F; s; son; no; Ft. Apache School, P.O. Ft. Apache, Apache Co, AZ; yes; *(Blank)*
3092; Hoskie Nas Woody; m; 7 (1925); F; s; son; yes; yes; *(Blank)*
3093; Si Doth Li Bahhe Hoske De Wood; m; 6 (1926); F; s; son; yes; yes; 329

3094; Wood; m; ?; F; m; Head; yes; yes; 4203
3095; Ne Bah; f; 22 (1910); F; m; wife; yes; yes; 4201
3096; aha Naz Bah; f; 20 (1912); F; m; wife; yes; yes; 4202
3097; Sikan Yellow Horse Jason; m; 17 (1905); F; s; son; yes; yes; 4469
3098; Ye Nez Bah; f; 4 (1928); F; s; dau; yes; yes; 4465

3099; Woody, Benjamin; m; 22 (1910); F; m; Head; yes; yes; *(Blank)*
3100; Way Yazza; f; 20 (1912); F; m; wife; yes; yes; 211
*3102;James, Benjamin; m; 4 (1928); F; s; son; yes; yes; 212
3103; Yazza Ada; f; 3 (1929); F; s; dau; yes; yes; 1156
           (*NOTE: #3101 was omitted on original)

*3103; Worker Bega; m; 30 (1902); F; m; Head; yes; yes; 3347
3104; Hosteen Ah She Bitse; f; 28 (1904); F; m; wife; yes; yes; 3348
3105; Ye Ni Bah; f; 10 (1922); F; s; dau; yes; yes; 3349
           (*NOTE: #3103 was listed twice)

3106; Worker Begay; m; 30 (1902); F; m; Head; yes; yes; *(Blank)*
3107; Worker Begay's Wife; f; 27 (1905); F; m; wife; yes; yes; *(Blank)*
3108; Gee Zine; f; 12 (1920); F; s; dau; yes; yes; *(Blank)*
3109; Ye Ne Bah; f; 10 (1922); F; s; dau; yes; yes; *(Blank)*

NAVAJO INDIAN CENSUS, (As of April 1, 1932)
KEY: Census Number; Name; Sex; Age at Last Birthday; Tribe (Navajo, unless otherwise stated); Degree of Blood; Marital Status; Relationship to Head of Family; At Jurisdiction where enrolled [Yes or No] (If no, Where); Ward [Yes or No]; Allotment, Annuity, and Identification Numbers.

3110; Kee Tso; m; 7 (1925); F; s; son; yes; yes; *(Blank)*
3111; Sh Le Ne; m; 3 (1929); F; s; son; yes; yes; *(Blank)*

3112; Ya, Joe; m; 26 (1906); F; m; Head; yes; yes; 1361
3113; Ye Dis Bah; f; 23 (1909); F; m; wife; yes; yes; 829
3114; Ye De Bah; f; 8 (1924); F; s; dau; yes; yes; 830
3115; Nellie; f; 5 (1927); F; s; dau; yes; yes; 1363

3116; Yah De Wood; m; 27 (1905); F; w; Head; yes; yes; *(Blank)*
3117; Aszan Ha Nu Chary; f; 9 (1923); F; s; dau; yes; yes; 5886

3118; Ya Na Ani De Yaz; m; 24 (1908); F; w; Head; yes; yes; *(Blank)*

3119; Yah Na Ne, Aszan; m; 53 (1879); F; m; Head; yes; yes; *(Blank)*
3120; Aha Na O To; f; 63 (1869); F; m; wife; yes; yes; *(Blank)*
3121; Helen; f; ?; F; s; dau; yes; yes; *(Blank)*

3122; Ye Si Si Bega, Hosteen; m; 33 (1899); F; m; Head; yes; yes; 1537
3123; Bitsi, Sarah; f; 28 (1904); F; m; wife; yes; yes; 1538
3124; Hoskie Ya Nan To; m; 11 (1921); F; s; son; yes; yes; 1664
3125; Kee Socie; m; 6 (1926); f; s; son; yes; yes; 1539
3126; Ad Aye Ah Si Violet Simpson; f; 4 (1928); F; s; dau; yes; yes; 1540
3127; Bahhe, Roy; m; 2 (1930); F; s; son; yes; yes; 1665

3128; Yazza Bitsey, Hosteen; f; 28 (1904); F; s; Head; yes; yes; 4046

3129; Yazza, Aszan; m; 63 (1869); F; w; Head; yes; yes; 437
3130; Si Chille; m; 33 (1899); F; s; son; yes; yes; *(Blank)*
3131; Nez, Sam; m; 31 (1901); F; s; son; yes; yes; *(Blank)*

3132; Yazza Begay; m; 30 (1902); F; m; Head; yes; yes; *(Blank)*
3133; Ye Na Yah Benna; f; 31 (1901); F; m; wife; yes; yes; 1452
3134; Ye Na Yah; m; 8 (1924); F; s; son; yes; yes; 1454
3135; Hoskie Na Da; m; 6 (1926); F; s; son; yes; yes; 1453
3136; Hoskie Na Das; m; 4 (1928); F; s; son; yes; yes; 1455

3137; Yazza, Dicker; m; 33 (1899); F; w; Head; yes; yes; *(Blank)*
3138; Oscar; m; 23 (1909); F; s; ?; yes; yes; *(Blank)*

3139; Yazza Hostine; m; 59 (1873); F; m; Head; yes; yes; 5811
3140; Bah; f; 41 (1881); F; m; wife; yes; yes; 6442

3141; Yazza, Hosteen; m; 38 (1894); F; m; Head; yes; yes; 5896
3142; Hosteen Yazza Bay Aszan; f; 38 (1894); F; m; wife; yes; yes; 5857

NAVAJO INDIAN CENSUS, (As of April 1, 1932)
KEY: Census Number; Name; Sex; Age at Last Birthday; Tribe (Navajo, unless otherwise stated); Degree of Blood; Marital Status; Relationship to Head of Family; At Jurisdiction where enrolled [Yes or No] (If no, Where); Ward [Yes or No]; Allotment, Annuity, and Identification Numbers.

3143; Hosteen Yazza; m; 19 (1913); F; s; son; yes; yes; 5921
3144; Dallas Eschon; m; 17 (1915); F; s; son; yes; yes; 5858
3145; Ah Ade Yazza; f; 15 (1917); F; s; dau; yes; yes; 5859
3146; Bah; f; 10 (1922); F; s; dau; yes; yes; 5860
3147; Ye Des Wood; m; 7 (1925); F; s; son; yes; yes; 5861
3148; Ye Des Bah; f; 5 (1927); F; s; dau; yes; yes; 5862
3149; Ne Ka Ta Day Wood; m; 3 (1929); F; s; son; yes; yes; 6067
3150; Isda, Lorenzo; m; 2 (1930); F; s; son; yes; yes; 6068
*3152; Ah De Chi; f; 63 (1869); F; m; wife; #2; yes; yes; 5865
3153; Aszan Nez; f; 23 (1909); F; s; grnd-dau; yes; yes; *(Blank)*
3154; Yahhe Wood; m; 6 (1926); F; s; grnd-son; yes; yes; 5867
3155; Shonie; m; 19 (1913); F; s; son; yes; yes; 5901
3156; Kina Big Gamber[sic]; f; 20 (1912); F; s; dau; yes; yes; 5866
#3156; Big Gambler, Andrew; m; 33 (1899); F; s; son; yes; yes; *(Blank)*
3157; Leawah Big Gambler; m; 29 (1903); F; s; son; yes; yes; *(Blank)*
3158; Big Gambler, Sam; m; 19 (1913); F; s; son; yes; yes; *(Blank)*
3159; Shepherd, Wesley; m; 22 (1910); F; s; son; yes; yes; 5868
3160; Se Le Bahhe; m; 10 (1922); F; s; son; yes; yes; 5869
3161; They Wood; m; 6 (1926); F; s; son; yes; yes; 3063
3162; Kee Kai; m; 2 (1930); F; s; son; yes; yes; 4593

(*NOTE: #3151 omitted on original) *(#NOTE: This number listed twice.)*

3163; Yazza, Hosteen; m; ?; F; m; Head; yes; yes; 582
3164; Away Yazze Bema; f; 29 (1903); F; m; wife; yes; yes; 826
3165; Morris; m; 11 (1921); F; s; son; yes; yes; 1362
3166; Away Yazze; f; 8 (1924); F; s; dau; yes; yes; 827
3167; Zani Yazze; f; 6 (1926); F; s; dau; yes; yes; 828

3168; Yazza, Hosteen; m; 37 (1895); F; m; Head; yes; yes; 1662
3169; Hosteen Yazza's Wife; f; 22 (1910); F; m; wife; yes; yes; 1553
3170; Zoni; f; 6 (1926); F; s; dau; yes; yes; 1554
3171; Chee; m; 3 (1929); F; s; son; yes; yes; 1555
3172; Ah Gee Kee, Jacob; m; 11 (1921); F; s; ?; yes; yes; *(Blank)*
3173; Denna Yazza; m; 10 (1922); F; s; ?; yes; yes; *(Blank)*
3174; Denna Soi; m; 8 (1924); F; s; ?; yes; yes; 1556
3175; Ta Chene Ha Socie; m; 23 (1909); F; s; ?; 206
3176; Hacke Bahhe; m; 2 (1930); F; s; son; yes; yes; 1660

3177; Yazza, Hosteen; m; 51 (1881); F; m; Head; yes; yes; *(Blank)*
3178; Aszan Nez; f; 38 (1894); F; m; wife; yes; yes; *(Blank)*

3179; Yazza, Hosteen; m; 45 (1887); F; m; Head; yes; yes; 6072
3180; Aszan Bahhe; f; 37 (1895); F; m; wife; yes; yes; 5783
3181; Yazza; m; 16 (1916); F; s; son; yes; yes; 6071

NAVAJO INDIAN CENSUS, (As of April 1, 1932)
KEY: Census Number; Name; Sex; Age at Last Birthday; Tribe (Navajo, unless otherwise stated); Degree of Blood; Marital Status; Relationship to Head of Family; At Jurisdiction where enrolled [Yes or No] (If no, Where); Ward [Yes or No]; Allotment, Annuity, and Identification Numbers.

3182; White Hair, Ralph; m; 13 (1919); F; s; son; yes; yes; 5784
3183; Kee; m; 8 (1924); F; s; son; yes; yes; 5785
3184; Si Si; f; 6 (1926); F; s; dau; yes; yes; 5786
3185; Aszan Nez; f; 2 (1930); F; s; dau; yes; yes; 6073
3186; Aszan Sihe; f; 23 (1909); F; m; wife #2; yes; yes; 5787
3187; Bahha; m; 13 (1919); F; s; son; yes; yes; 5863
3188; Bahhe; f; 8 (1924); F; s; dau; yes; yes; 5789
3189; Hoskie Yazza; m; 5 (1927); F; s; son; yes; yes; 5790
3190; Aszan; f; 3 (1929); F; s; dau; yes; yes; 5791
3191; Hoskie Yazza; m; 2 (1930); F; s; son; yes; yes; 6070

3192; Yazza, Howard; m; 34 (1898); F; w; Head; yes; yes; 3560

3193; Yazza Na Chene; m; 49 (1883); F; m; Head; yes; yes; 3850
3194; Yazza Chene's Wife; f; 43 (1889); F; m; wife; yes; yes; 3851
3195; Ethel; f; 19 (1913); F; s; dau; yes; yes; 3852
3196; Yazzie Away; f; 11 (1921); F; s; dau; yes; yes; 3853
3197; Yazza Ach; m; 7 (1925); F; s; son; yes; yes; 3854
3198; Dah Ton Ha; f; 5 (1927); F; s; dau; yes; yes; 3855
3199; Yazza Nachehe Wife #2; f; 22 (1910); F; m; wife; yes; yes; 3856
3200; Gulic Nah; f; 6 (1926); F; s; dau; yes; yes; *(Blank)*
3201; Yazza Kee; m; 4 (1928); F; s; son; yes; yes; *(Blank)*

3202; Yazze, Aszan; f; 63 (1869); F; w; Head; yes; yes; 19

3203; Yazza, Aszan; f; 23 (1909); F; w; Head; yes; yes; 182
3204; Kee Socie; f; 5 (1927); F; s; dau; yes; yes;183
3205; Has Bah; f; 3 (1920); F; s; dau; yes; yes; 934

3206; Yazze, Aszan; f; 62 (1870); F; w; Head; yes; yes; 786
3207; Denna Yazze; m; 14 (1918); F; s; grnd-son; yes; yes; 787
3208; Bah; f; 9 (1923); F; s; grnd-dau; yes; yes; 788
3209; Hosteen Guy; m; 9 (1923); F; s; nephew; yes; yes; *(Blank)*

3210; Yazze, Bahhe; f; 38 (1894); F; w; Head; yes; yes; 284
3211; Dena Socie, Richard; m; 18 (1914); F; s; son; no; Ft. Apache School, P.O. Ft. Apache, Apache Co, AZ; yes; 91
3212; Ah Sa Has Bah; f; 17 (1915); F; s; dau; yes; yes; 93
3213; Jennie; f; 14 (1918); F; s; dau; yes; yes; 92
3214; Aha Na Bah; f; 12 (1920); F; s; dau; yes; yes; *(Blank)*
3215; Bahhe; m; 9 (1923); F; s; son; yes; yes; *(Blank)*
3216; Bahhe Yazze; m; 7 (1925); F; s; son; yes; yes; 285
3217; Yah Ne Yazze; m; 4 (1928); F; s; son; yes; yes; 286

NAVAJO INDIAN CENSUS, (As of April 1, 1932)

KEY: Census Number; Name; Sex; Age at Last Birthday; Tribe (Navajo, unless otherwise stated); Degree of Blood; Marital Status; Relationship to Head of Family; At Jurisdiction where enrolled [Yes or No] (If no, Where); Ward [Yes or No]; Allotment, Annuity, and Identification Numbers.

3218; Yazze Bega, Hosteen; m; 29 (1903); F; m; Head; yes; yes; *(Blank)*
3219; Zani Guy; f; 29 (1903); F; m; wife; yes; yes; 291
3220; Ahs Ah Bah; f; 5 (1927); F; s; dau; yes; yes; 292

3221; Yazze, Hosteen; m; 27 (1895); F; m; Head; yes; yes; 130
3222; Clah Soi Bitsi; f; 25 (1907); F; m; wife; yes; yes; 132
3223; Yazze, George; m; 4 (1928); F; s; son; yes; yes; 131

3224; Yazze, Hosteen; m; ?; F; m; Head; yes; yes; *(Blank)*
3225; Aszan Si Na Jinne; f; 48 (1884); F; m; wife; yes; yes; 784
3226; Goth; m; 17 (1915); F; s; son; yes; yes; *(Blank)*
3227; Bah; f; 9 (1923); F; s; dau; yes; yes; 785

3228; Yazze, Hosteen; m; 56 (1876); F; m; Head; yes; yes; 837
3229; Yazze, Hosteen, Wife; f; 57 (1875); F; m; wife; yes; yes; 838
3230; Ye Ne Ye Bah Way Chee; f; 22 (1910); F; s; dau; yes; yes; 839
3231; Chonnie; m; 7 (1925); F; s; son; yes; yes; 840
3232; Clie Ne Bah; f; 8 (1924); F; s; dau; yes; yes; 841
3233; Ernest; m; 26 (1906); F; s; son; yes; yes; 867
3234; Clesn Yazze; m; 22 (1910); F; s; son; yes; yes; *(Blank)*

3235; Yazze, Hosteen; m; 32 (1900); F; m; Head; yes; yes; 2992
3236; Bah; f; 25 (1907); F; m; wife; yes; yes; 2993
3237; Kee Soi; m; 11 (1921); F; s; son; yes; yes; 2994
3238; Has Ne Hean; m; 8 (1924); F; s; son; yes; yes; *(Blank)*
3239; Dena Chee; m; 7 (1925); F; s; son; yes; yes; 3010
3240; Ah Ana Bah; f; 6 (1926); F; s; dau; yes; yes; 2995
3241; Toe De Cheene; m; 27 (1905); F; s; son; yes; yes; 2996
3242; Gee Toli Octavia Nez; f; 20 (1912); F; s; niece; yes; yes; 3361
3243; Charley; m; 23 (1909); F; s; ?; yes; yes; 2986

3244; Yazze To To Gene; m; 48 (1884); F; m; Head; yes; yes; 3573
3245; Taylor, Howard; m; 18 (1914); F; s; son; yes; yes; *(Blank)*
3246; Yazze; f; 33 (1899); F; s; wife; yes; yes; 3581
3247; Asafee Bah; f; 25 (1907); F; s; dau; yes; yes; 3578
3248; Hosteen; m; 25 (1907); F; s; son; yes; yes; 3580
3249; Sisco Aszan; f; 14 (1918); F; s; dau; yes; yes; 3584
3250; Zahn Nie Bah; f; 10 (1922); F; s; dau; yes; yes; 3586
3251; Ne Glenne Bah; f; 7 (1925); F; s; dau; yes; yes; 3588
3252; Ah He De Bah; f; 5 (1927); F; s; dau; yes; yes; 3585

3253; Yazzie Bahhe; m; 28 91904); F; m; Head; yes; yes; *(Blank)*
3254; Be Za De Bega #2; f; 19 (1913); F; m; wife; yes; yes; *(Blank)*
3255; Dah De Bah; f; 3 (1929); F; s; dau; yes; yes; 5797

NAVAJO INDIAN CENSUS, (As of April 1, 1932)

KEY: Census Number; Name; Sex; Age at Last Birthday; Tribe (Navajo, unless otherwise stated); Degree of Blood; Marital Status; Relationship to Head of Family; At Jurisdiction where enrolled [Yes or No] (If no, Where); Ward [Yes or No]; Allotment, Annuity, and Identification Numbers.

3256; Aszan Coy; f; 36 (1894); F; s; dau; yes; yes; 5799
    (NOTE: The above entry is copied as is on original)

3257; Yazzie Hosteen; m; 53 (1879); F; m; Head; yes; yes; *(Blank)*
3258; Ruth; f; 25 (1907); F; m; wife; yes; yes; 3689

3259; Yellow Hair; m; 37 (1895); F; m; Head; yes; yes; *(Blank)*
3260; Ade Bahhe; f; 21 (1911); F; m; wife; yes; yes; *(Blank)*
3261; Kee Yazza; m; 5 (1927); F; s; son; yes; yes; *(Blank)*

3262; Yellow Hair; m; ?; F; w; Head; yes; yes; 144

3263; Yellow Hair; m; 45 (1887); F; m; Head; yes; yes; 3591
3264; Yellow Horse's Daughter; f; 36 (1896); F; m; wife; yes; yes; 3592
3265; Nah Chet; m; 19 (1913); F; s; son; yes; yes; 4138
3266; May; f; 16 (1916); F; s; dau; yes; yes; 3711
3267; Lottie; f; 13 (1919); F; s; dau; yes; yes; 3712
3268; Yetas Bah; f; 6 (1926); F; s; dau; yes; yes; 3579
3269; Ha De Bah; f; 5 (1927); F; s; dau; yes; yes; 3578
3270; Marion; m; 15 (1917); F; s; son; yes; yes; 3577
3271; Dick; m; 4 (1928); F; s; son; yes; yes; 3576
3272; Yazzie; m; 38 (1894); F; s; ?; yes; yes; *(Blank)*

3273; Yellow Hair's Brother-in-Law; m; 48 (1884); F; w; Head; yes; yes; *(Blank)*
3274; George; m; 16 (1916); F; s; son; yes; yes; 6367

3275; Yellow Hair, Mary; f; 20 (1912); F; w; Head; yes; yes; 5312
3276; Martha; f; 17 (1915); F; s; dau; yes; yes; 5309
3277; Ne Na Ges Bah; f; 12 (1920); F; s; dau; yes; yes; 2966

3278; Yellow Horse Begay; m; 33 (1899); F; m; Head; yes; yes; 3902
3279; De Da Wood Hoskie Benna; f; 30 (1902); F; m; wife; yes; yes; 3606
3280; Dade Wood Hoskie; m; 8 (1924); F; s; son; yes; yes; 3607

3281; Yellow Horse's Daughter #1; f; 58 (1874); F; w; Head; yes; yes; 3572
3282; Esky, Mike; m; 27 (1905); F; s; son; yes; yes; 3571

3283; Yellow Horse #1; m; 87 (1845); F; m; Head; yes; yes; 3601
3284; Yellow Horse's Wife; f; 68 (1864); F; m; wife; yes; yes; 3696
3285; Bah Chenna; f; 18 (1914); F; s; grnd-dau; yes; yes; 3597
3286; Nina; f; 13 (1919); F; s; grnd-dau; yes; yes; 3598
3287; Chee Nez; f; 10 (1922); F; s; grnd-dau; yes; yes; 3599
3288; Des Dah Ade; f; 8 (1924); F; s; grnd-dau; yes; yes; 3600

NAVAJO INDIAN CENSUS, (As of April 1, 1932)
KEY: Census Number; Name; Sex; Age at Last Birthday; Tribe (Navajo, unless otherwise stated); Degree of Blood; Marital Status; Relationship to Head of Family; At Jurisdiction where enrolled [Yes or No] (If no, Where); Ward [Yes or No]; Allotment, Annuity, and Identification Numbers.

3289; Yellow Horse's Grand-daughter; f; 22 (1910); F; w; Head; yes; yes; 3791
3290; Zahn Gray, Rosaline; f; 8 (1924); F; s; dau; yes; yes; 3801
3291; Nez Hosteen; m; 45 (1887); F; s; bro; yes; yes; 3792

3292; Yellow Horse's Grand-son; m; 25 (1907); F; m; Head; yes; yes; *(Blank)*
3293; Za Chi Bah; f; 16 (1916); F; m; wife; yes; yes; 3893
3294; Kee Bahhe; m; 3 (1929); F; s; son; yes; yes; 4466

3295; Yellow Horse's Son #1; m; 39 (1893); F; m; Head; yes; yes; 5615
3296; Hosk Con Bitsey; f; 41 (1891); F; m; wife; yes; yes; 5616
3297; Timothy; m; 18 (1914); F; s; son; yes; yes; 6022
3298; Lorene; f; 15 (1917); F; s; dau; yes; yes; 5618
3299; Oscine; m; 7 (1925); F; s; son; yes; yes; 5619
3300; Yazza Away; f; 5 (1927); F; s; dau; yes; yes; 5620
3301; Hoskie Bahhe Benna; f; 25 (1907); F; s; wife #2; yes; yes; 5621
3302; Hoskie Bahhe; m; 3 (1929); F; s; son; yes; yes; 5622

3303; Yellow Horse's Son; m; ?; F; m; Head; yes; yes; 569
3304; Bah; f; 23 (1909); F; m; wife; yes; yes; 561
3305; Aszan Has Len; f; 8 (1924); F; s; dau; yes; yes; 562
3306; Denet Bahhe; f; 6 (1926); F; s; dau; yes; yes; 563

3307; Yee He Yai; m; 36 (1896); F; m; Head; yes; yes; 248
3308; Aszan Bah; f; 32 (1900); F; m; wife; yes; yes; 249
3309; Ye Nez Bah; f; 7 (1925); F; s; dau; yes; yes; 250
3310; Emma; f; 4 (1928); F; s; dau; yes; yes; 252
3311; Julian; m; 13 (1919); F; s; stp-son; yes; yes; 1695
3312; Ne Chonne; f; 26 (1906); F; m; wife #2; yes; yes; 258
3313; Ne Nas Bah; f; 8 (1924); F; s; dau; yes; yes; 257

3314; Yees Na; f; ?; F; w; Head; yes; yes; *(Blank)*

3315; Yo En Tellie Bega, Hosteen; m; 28 (1904); F; m; Head; yes; yes; *(Blank)*
3316; Zannie Jinnie Socie, Betsie; f; 30 (1903); 193
3317; Ah Che Ne Ne Bah; f; 21 (1911); F; s; dau; yes; yes; 194
3318; Soi; m; 9 (1923); F; s; son; yes; yes; *(Blank)*
3319; Ne; m; 7 (1925); F; s; son; yes; yes; 436
3320; Cli Ahs Na Bah; f; 4 (1928); F; s; dau; yes; yes; 195

3321; Yo En Tilli, Hosteen, Wife; f; 57 (1875); F; w; Head; yes; yes; 112
3322; Chelley Bema; f; 24 (1908); F; w; dau; yes; yes; 138
3323; Hosteen Cle Chee; m; 7 (1925); F; s; grnd-son; yes; yes; 127
3324; May; f; 9 (1923); F; s; grnd-dau; yes; yes; 134
3325; Zah, Henry; m; 22 (1910); F; s; son; yes; yes; 955

NAVAJO INDIAN CENSUS, (As of April 1, 1932)
KEY: Census Number; Name; Sex; Age at Last Birthday; Tribe (Navajo, unless otherwise stated); Degree of Blood; Marital Status; Relationship to Head of Family; At Jurisdiction where enrolled [Yes or No] (If no, Where); Ward [Yes or No]; Allotment, Annuity, and Identification Numbers.

3326; Yo En Tillie, Wilson; m; 14 (1918); F; s; grnd-son; yes; yes; 956

3327; Yo Cuh Ne Bah; m; 68 (1864); F; m; Head; yes; yes; 1550
3328; Bah; f; 32 (1900); F; m; wife; yes; yes; 1473
3329; Aszan Tahhe; f; 4 (1928); F; s; dau; yes; yes; 1636

3330; Ysuenthe Beta, Hosteen; m; 43 (1889); F; m; Head; yes; yes; *(Blank)*
3331; Yo Unso Bema; f; 33 (1899); F; m; wife; yes; yes; 3921
3332; Yo Unso; m; 9 (1923); F; s; son; yes; yes; 3924
3333; Wholla; m; 6 (1926); F; s; son; yes; yes; 3922
3334; Use Chilly; m; 4 (1928); F; s; son; yes; yes; 3923

3335; Yus Bah; f; 18 (1914); F; w; Head; yes; yes; 48

3336; Zahn Chene Begay; m; 105 (1827); F; m; Head; yes; yes; 3813
3337; Zahn Chene Bema; f; 25 (1907); F; m; wife; yes; yes; 3814
3338; Ad Ade Soc; f; 10 (1922); F; s; dau; yes; yes; *(Blank)*
3339; Zahn Chene; f; 8 (1924); F; s; dau; yes; yes; 3815
3340; Yazzie Zahn; f; 6 (1926); F; s; dau; yes; yes; 3816
3341; Bahhe Aszan; f; 4 (1928); F; s; dau; yes; yes; 3817

3342; Zahns Dahs; f; 63 (1869); F; w; Head; yes; yes; *(Blank)*

3343; Zah Nez Socie Beda; m; 32 (1900); F; m; Head; yes; yes; 4027
3344; See See; f; 19 (1913); F; m; wife; yes; yes; 4018
3345; Yazza; m; 35 (1897); F; s; ?; yes; yes; *(Blank)*

3346; Zah Nez Soice Bega; m; 31 (1901); F; w; Head; yes; yes; 4045

3347; Zahns Gy Bega; m; 39 (1893); F; m; Head; yes; yes; *(Blank)*
3348; Sangster, Sybil; f; 23 (1909); F; m; wife; yes; yes; *(Blank)*
3349; Joe; m; 18 (1914); F; s; ?; yes; yes; *(Blank)*

3350; Zani, Bah; f; 79 (1853); F; w; Head; yes; yes; 207

3351; Zenah Va He, Joe John; m; ?; F; m; Head; yes; yes; 4451
3352; Zenah Bah Aszan; f; 53 (1879); F; m; wife; yes; yes; 4403
3353; Zenah Bay Bitsey; f; 26 (1906); F; m; wife; yes; yes; 4304

3354; Ze Na Jinny; m; 53 (1879); F; w; Head; yes; yes; *(Blank)*

3355; Zinni Jinny Bega; m; 41 (1891); F; m; Head; yes; yes; *(Blank)*
3356; Aszan Yazze; f; 39 (1893); F; m; wife; yes; yes; 791
3357; Ah Ade Yazze; f; 18 (1914); F; s; dau; yes; yes; *(Blank)*

NAVAJO INDIAN CENSUS, (As of April 1, 1932)
KEY: Census Number; Name; Sex; Age at Last Birthday; Tribe (Navajo, unless otherwise stated); Degree of Blood; Marital Status; Relationship to Head of Family; At Jurisdiction where enrolled [Yes or No] (If no, Where); Ward [Yes or No]; Allotment, Annuity, and Identification Numbers.

3358; Aha Has Bah; f; 20 (1912); F; s; dau; yes; yes; 792
3359; Denet Bahhe; m; 16 (1916); f; s; son; yes; yes; *(Blank)*
3360; Gath; m; 14 (1918); F; s; son; yes; yes; *(Blank)*
3361; Bini Key; m; 10 (1922); F; s; son; no; Leupp School, P.O. Leupp, Coconino Co, AZ; yes; *(Blank)*
3362; E He; m; 11 (1921); F; s; son; yes; yes; *(Blank)*
3363; Nas Bah; f; 9 (1923); F; s; dau; yes; yes; 793
3364; Gath Li; m; 8 (1924); F; s; son; yes; yes; 794
3365; Kee An Na Si He; f; 5 (1927); F; s; dau; yes; yes; 795

3366; Zinny, Aszan; f; 93 (1839); F; w; Head; yes; yes; 557

3367; Zith Clah Ne; m; ?; F; m; Head; yes; yes; 1606
3368; Kee Chee; m; 7 (1925); F; s; nephew; yes; yes; 1493
3369; Ath Ne Bah; f; 3 (1929); F; s; dau; yes; yes; 4640
3370; Kee Da Soui; m; 6 (1926); F; s; son; yes; yes; 1494
3371; No Have Zha; m; 2 (1930); F; s; son; yes; yes; 1605

3372; Zoni Kay Kenny; m; ?; F; w; Head; yes; yes; *(Blank)*
3373; Dennis; m; 11 (1921); F; s; son; yes; yes; *(Blank)*
3374; Dah Nah Bah; f; 7 (1925); F; s; dau; yes; yes; 1534
3375; Chee Ye, Ethel; f; 12 (1920); F; s; dau; yes; yes; *(Blank)*
3376; Ah Be Chi, Melvin; m; ?; F; s; son; yes; yes; *(Blank)*
3377; Lola; f; 16 (1916); F; s; dau; yes; yes; *(Blank)*

3378; Zuni, Jinney; m; 39 (1893); F; m; Head; yes; yes; 3716
3379; Zuni's, Jinney, Wife; f; 39 (1893); F; m; wife; yes; yes; 3717
3380; Chonnie; f; 21 (1911); F; s; wife; yes; yes; 3718

3381; Zuni Jinney; m; 41 (1891); F; m; Head; yes; yes; 70
3382; Zuni Jinney Bah Aszan; f; 26 (1906); F; m; wife; yes; yes; 313
3383; Aszan Chee; f; 5 (1927); F; s; dau; yes; yes; 314

3384; Zuni Jinney Begay; m; 38 (1894); F; m; Head; yes; yes; 904
3385; Cay Wood Benna; f; 36 (1896); F; m; wife; yes; yes; 900
3386; Cay Wood; m; 16 (1916); F; s; son; yes; yes; *(Blank)*
3387; Ye Nes Bah; f; 11 (1921); F; s; dau; yes; yes; 901
3388; Kee Se Ne; m; 9 (1923); F; s; son; yes; yes; *(Blank)*
3389; Gee; m; 8 (1924); F; s; son; yes; yes; 902
3390; Ne Gees Bah; f; 4 (1928); F; s; dau; yes; yes; 903
3391; Ada Kai; f; 3 (1929); F; s; dau; yes; yes; 1165
3392; Has Bah Tsitnot Jinnie; f; 2 (1930); F; s; dau; yes; yes; *(Blank)*

NAVAJO INDIAN CENSUS, (As of April 1, 1932)

KEY: Census Number; Name; Sex; Age at Last Birthday; Tribe (Navajo, unless otherwise stated); Degree of Blood; Marital Status; Relationship to Head of Family; At Jurisdiction where enrolled [Yes or No] (If no, Where); Ward [Yes or No]; Allotment, Annuity, and Identification Numbers.

3393; Zuni Jinney Sonni Bitsi; f; 43 (1889); F; w; Head; yes; yes; 895
3394; Hoskie Ta Des Wood, Raymond; m; 17 (1915); F; s; son; yes; yes; 896
3395; Minnie; f; 8 (1924); F; s; dau; yes; yes; 899

3396; Zuni Jinny; m; 34 (1898); F; m; Head; yes; yes; *(Blank)*
3397; Ha Nes Bah; f; 28 (1904); F; m; wife; yes; yes; 3331
3398; Kee Yazza; m; 5 (1927); F; s; son; yes; yes; 3332
3399; Kee Bahhe; m; 7 (1925); F; s; son; yes; yes; 3333
3400; Tolle; m; 19 (1913); F; s; bro; yes; yes; 3330

3401; Zuni Jinny Badone; m; ?; F m; Head; yes; yes; *(Blank)*
3402; Baszan Yazze; f; 41 (1891); F; m; wife; yes; yes; 885
3403; Zhuni; m; 12 (1920); F; s; son; yes; yes; *(Blank)*

3404; Zuni Jinny Sonni; m; 85 (1847); F; m; Head; yes; yes; 884
3405; Zuni Jinny Sonni's Wife; f; 74 (1858); F; m; wife; yes; yes; 888
3406; Hoskie Kee Nas Wood; m; 32 (1900); F; s; son; yes; yes; *(Blank)*

3407; Zuni Jinny Soue; m; 56 (1876); F; w; Head; yes; yes; 356

LIVE BIRTHS
of the
NAVAJO TRIBE
Hopi Indian Agency

Keams Canon,

Arizona 1929 - 1931

LIVE BIRTHS, (Occurring between July 1, 1929, and June 30, 1930)
KEY: 1930 Census Roll Number ("----" indicates no number given); Name; *Date of Birth (1929); Sex; Tribe (Navajo, unless otherwise indicated); Ward [yes or no]; Degree of Father's blood; Degree of Mother's blood; Degree of Child's blood; At jurisdiction where enrolled [yes or no]; (If "no", where?). *(*NOTE: No exact birthdate given for any of the entries, "Born During Fiscal Year 1929" is the only date given.)*

35; Can; 1929; f; yes; F; F; F; yes

42; Thani; 1929; m; yes; F; F; F; yes

74; Ah De Chi, Lorenzo; 1929; m; yes; F; F; F; yes

177; Na Glen; 1929; f; yes; F; F; F; yes

212; Aszan Sispe; 1929; f; yes; F; F; F; yes

295; Tollie; 1929; f; yes; F; F; F; yes

304; Bay Yazzie; 1929; f; yes; F; F; F; yes

355; Yell Wood De; 1929; m; yes; F; F; F; yes

362; Kee Soi; 1929; m; yes; F; F; F; yes

455; Tollie; 1929; m; yes; F; F; F; yes

465; Denna Kai; 1929; m; yes; F; F; F; yes

486; Kee Chee; 1929; m; yes; F; F; F; yes

531; Haske Haswood; 1929; m; yes; F; F; F; yes

629; Bitsey Begay's Daughter, Jane; 1929; f; yes; F; F; F; yes

662; Way Soi; 1929; m; yes; F; F; F; yes

763; Peterson, Gloria; 1929; f; yes; F; F; F; yes

779; Denna Guy; 1929; m; yes; F; F; F; yes

827; Da Yezzie; 1929; f; yes; F; F; F; yes

909; Sh Way; 1929; m; yes; F; F; F; yes

921; Hosk The Ne Yah; 1929; m; yes; F; F; F; yes

929; Bahhe, Ada; 1929; f; yes; F; F; F; yes

LIVE BIRTHS, (Occurring between July 1, 1929, and June 30, 1930)

KEY: 1930 Census Roll Number ("----" indicates no number given); Name; *Date of Birth (1929); Sex; Tribe (Navajo, unless otherwise indicated); Ward [yes or no]; Degree of Father's blood; Degree of Mother's blood; Degree of Child's blood; At jurisdiction where enrolled [yes or no]; (If "no", where?). *(*NOTE: No exact birthdate given for any of the entries, "Born During Fiscal Year 1929" is the only date given.)*

962; Ah Bae; 1929; f; yes; F; F; F; yes

969; Zahn Kai; 1929; f; yes; F; F; F; yes

997; Clony Zanni, Bessie; 1929; f; yes; F; F; F; yes

998; Clony Zanni, Elsie; 1929; f; yes; F; F; F; yes

1003; Ye De Bah, Bessie Rope; 1929; f; yes; F; F; F; yes

1025; Bahhe Na Zoing; 1929; f; yes; F; F; F; yes

1063; Na La Yezzie; 1929; m; yes; F; F; F; yes

1086; Dennea Sini Cate He; 1929; m; yes; F; F; F; yes

2100; Bitone Chee; 1929; m; yes; F; F; F; yes *(**NOTE:** Numbered as is on original.)*

1217; Na Glen Ta Ne; 1929; f; yes; F; F; F; yes

1239; Hoskie Beel; 1929; m; yes; F; F; F; yes

1533; Frank, May; 1929; f; yes; F; F; F; yes

1539; Hos Che Yazzie; 1929; m; yes; F; F; F; yes

1684; Bahhe, Roy; 1929; m; yes; F; F; F; yes

1692; Haloni Beda, Paul; 1929; m; yes; F; F; F; yes

1739; Ye Ne Wood; 1929; m; yes; F; F; F; yes

1817; Yazze, Ada; 1929; f; yes; F; F; F; yes

1830; Lat, Bessie; 1929; f; yes; F; F; F; yes

2029; Ne Pah Ye Ne Yea; 1929; m; yes; F; F; F; yes

2120; Ah Gee Bah; 1929; f; yes; F; F; F; yes

2171; Denna Chee; 1929; m; yes; F; F; F; yes

LIVE BIRTHS, (Occurring between July 1, 1929, and June 30, 1930)

KEY: 1930 Census Roll Number ("----" indicates no number given); Name; *Date of Birth (1929); Sex; Tribe (Navajo, unless otherwise indicated); Ward [yes or no]; Degree of Father's blood; Degree of Mother's blood; Degree of Child's blood; At jurisdiction where enrolled [yes or no]; (If "no", where?). *(*NOTE: No exact birthdate given for any of the entries, "Born During Fiscal Year 1929" is the only date given.)*

2195; Woody; 1929; m; yes; F; F; F; yes

2277; La Ne Zinne; 1929; m; yes; F; F; F; yes

2321; Gis Chone De; 1929; f; yes; F; F; F; yes

2337; Hoskie; 1929; m; yes; F; F; F; yes

NOTE: The following names were overlooked when making records. Birth certificates that could not be located on Birth Rolls:

KEY: Name; Date of Birth; Sex; Tribe [Navajo]; Mother's Name; Father's Name; At Jurisdiction where enrolled [yes or no]; Residence or Place of Birth.

Nez, Mae; 1-27-1929; f; Gertrude Jashivenka; Wilson; yes; Navajo Co, Hoteville, AZ

Wood, Yend; 5-?-1929; m; Betty Smith; Unknown; yes; Navajo Co, Hoteville, AZ
(Ileig written beside name)

Ne Te, Hostee; 3-5-1930; m; Pearl Aszan, George; yes; Navajo Co, ?, AZ

Nelson, [Reported as Chas]; 10-29-1930; m; Irene Nelson; Charley Watchman; yes; Navajo Co, Keams Canyon, AZ
(Stillborn and Ileig written beside name)

Nemore, Dennet; 3-1-1930; m; Ahade Soice; Hosteen Be Za; yes; Navajo Co, ?, AZ

Peterson, Gloria; 3-3-1930; f; Rosie ?; Herman; yes; Navajo Co, ?, AZ

LIVE BIRTHS, (Occurring between April 1, 1930, and March 31, 1931)
KEY: 1931 Census Roll Number ("----" indicates no number given); Name; *Date of Birth (1930); Sex; Tribe (Navajo, unless otherwise indicated); Ward [yes or no]; Degree of Father's blood; Degree of Mother's blood; Degree of Child's blood; At jurisdiction where enrolled [yes or no]; (If "no", where?). *(*NOTE: No exact birthdate given for any of the entries, "Born During Fiscal Year 1930" is the only date given.)*

20; Ne The He Wood; 1930; m; yes; F; F; F; yes

27; Yazzie John; 1930; m; yes; F; F; F; yes

69; Dena Soi; 1930; m; yes; F; F; F; yes

75; Kee Soise He; 1930; m; yes; F; F; F; yes

178; Hoskie Sile; 1930; m; yes; F; F; F; yes

242; Hoskie Ne She Ye, King; 1930; m; yes; F; F; F; yes

318; Chee Bahhe; 1930; m; yes; F; F; F; yes

325; Hoskee Yazzie; 1930; m; yes; F; F; F; yes

379; Duna Ne Mozzie; 1930; m; yes; F; F; F; yes

487; Tane Bah Yazzie; 1930; F; yes; F; F; F; yes

593; Billy, Mary; 1930; f; yes; F; F; F; yes

597; Lavo, John; 1930; m; yes; F; F; F; yes

654; Hosteen Socie Yazzie; 1930; m; yes; F; F; F; yes

675; Black Man's Son, Billy; 1930; m; yes; F; F; F; yes

707; Al Di De Bah; 1930; f; yes; F; F; F; yes

765; Hoskie; 1930; m; yes; F; F; F; yes

1073; Way She He; 1930; m; yes; F; F; F; yes

1104; Hoskie; 1930; m; yes; F; F; F; yes

1196; Bahhe, Ada; 1930; f; yes; F; F; F; yes

1400; Denna Ach He; 1930; m; yes; F; F; F; yes

1605; Hosk Ni Con; 1930; m; yes; F; F; F; yes

LIVE BIRTHS, (Occurring between April 1, 1930, and March 31, 1931)
KEY: 1931 Census Roll Number ("----" indicates no number given); Name; *Date of Birth (1930); Sex; Tribe (Navajo, unless otherwise indicated); Ward [yes or no]; Degree of Father's blood; Degree of Mother's blood; Degree of Child's blood; At jurisdiction where enrolled [yes or no]; (If "no", where?). *(*NOTE: No exact birthdate given for any of the entries, "Born During Fiscal Year 1930" is the only date given.)*

1645; Gray Hat's Grandson, Bessie; 1930; f; yes; F; F; F; yes

1696; Ni Na Bah; 1930; f; yes; F; F; F; yes

1748; Zahn Chee; 1930; f; yes; F; F; F; yes

1869; Izzy Nez Bega, Joe; 1930; m; yes; F; F; F; yes

1981; Ye Ne Bah; 1930; f; yes; F; F; F; yes

2014; Tally, Frank; 1930; m; yes; F; F; F; yes

2075; Lewis, Jim; 1930; m; yes; F; F; F; yes

2081; Lewis, Laura; 1930; f; yes; F; F; F; yes

2131; Lewis, Tommy; 1930; m; yes; F; F; F; yes

2132; Lewis, Charley; 1930; m; yes; F; F; F; yes

2136; Bahhe, Ada; 1930; f; yes; F; F; F; yes

2343; Nelson, Annie; 1930; f; yes; F; F; F; yes

2366; Gee Zinni; 1930; m; yes; F; F; F; yes

2380; Nez Clanny Begay, Ross; 1930; m; yes; F; F; F; yes

2571; Robinson, Rosilie; 1930; f; yes; F; F; F; yes

2639; Ne Bah; 1930; f; yes; F; F; F; yes

2736; Hosk Ni Yap; 1930; m; yes; F; F; F; yes

2774; Away Yazzie; 1930; f; yes; F; F; F; yes

2793; Dema Ach He; 1930; m; yes; F; F; F; yes

2837; Be Cak Zi Bah; 1930; f; yes; F; F; F; yes

2968; Zahn Chee; 1930; f; yes; F; F; F; yes

LIVE BIRTHS. (Occurring between April 1, 1930, and March 31, 1931)
KEY: 1931 Census Roll Number ("----" indicates no number given); Name; *Date of Birth (1930); Sex; Tribe (Navajo, unless otherwise indicated); Ward [yes or no]; Degree of Father's blood; Degree of Mother's blood; Degree of Child's blood; At jurisdiction where enrolled [yes or no]; (If "no", where?). *(*NOTE: No exact birthdate given for any of the entries, "Born During Fiscal Year 1930" is the only date given.)*

2990; Al Sie He; 1930; m; yes; F; F; F; yes

3042; Soi Begay, Raymond; 1930; m; yes; F; F; F; yes

3068; Kan Soie; 1930; f; yes; F; F; F; yes

3207; Hoske Tahe; 1930; m; yes; F; F; F; yes

3320; Ne Ta Ye Tie; 1930; m; yes; F; F; F; yes

3379; Bahhe, Roy; 1930; m; yes; F; F; F; yes

3402; Ne La Ta Dey Wood, Lorenzo; 1930; m; yes; F; F; F; yes

3414; Kee Kai; 1930; f; yes; F; F; F; yes

3429; Hoske Bahhe; 1930; m; yes; F; F; F; yes

3438; Aszan Nez; 1930; f; yes; F; F; F; yes

3444; Hoskie Yazze; 1930; m; yes; F; F; F; yes

3629; No Have Zha; 1930; m; yes; F; F; F; yes

3651; Has Bah Tsitnot Jinnie; 1930; f; yes; F; F; F; yes

DEATHS

of the

NAVAJO TRIBE

Hopi Indian Agency

Keams Canon, Arizona

1930 - 1931

DEATHS, (Occurring between April 1, 1930, and March 31, 1931)
KEY: Number on 1930 Census Roll; Name; Date of Death; Age at Death; Sex; Tribe (Navajo, unless otherwise indicated); Ward [yes or no]; Degree of Blood; Cause of Death (if given); At jurisdiction where enrolled [yes or no]; (If "no", where?).

107;   Yah Ne Bah; ?-1930; 10 yr; f; yes; F; ?; yes

138;   Bah; ?-1930; ?; f; yes; F; ?; yes

199;   Tah Ne Bah; ?-1930; 6 yr; f; yes; F; ?; yes

214;   Sannie, Charlie; ?-1930; 82 yr; m; yes; F; ?; yes

218;   Bega #2 Wife; ?-1930; 23 yr; f; yes; F; ?; yes

227;   Dena Sosie; 3-1931; 2 yr; m; yes; F; ?; yes

324;   Sam B. Clara; ?-1930; ?; f; yes; F; ?; yes

548;   Yah Na Bah; 2-1931; 16 yr; f; yes; F; ?; yes

574;   Silversmith Jim's Wife; 7-5-1930; 55 yr; f; yes; F; ?; yes

613;   Chee; 5-12-1930; 8 yr; m; yes; F; ?; yes

640;   Hosteen Yo En Tilli; 2-1931; 83 yr; m; yes; F; ?; yes

654;   Dena Sosie; 6-3-1930; 10 yr; m; yes; F; yes

687;   Aszan Nez; ?-1930; 10 yr; m; yes; F; ?; yes

688;   Zan Nez Clanny; 8-19-1930; 51 yr; m; yes; F; ?; yes

743;   Blacksheep; 5-1930; ?; m; yes; F; Heart failure; yes

840;   Zani Se He, Mary; 2-2-1930; 12 yr; f; yes; F; ?; yes

910;   Ya Ha Bah; ?-1930; 29 yr; f; yes; F; ?; yes

976;   Frank's Wife; ?-1930-31; 21 yr; f; yes; F; ?; yes

984;   Do Ha Bah; ?-1930; 3 yr; f; yes; F; ?; yes

1083; Taus Bah; 4-11-1930; 18 yr; f; yes; F; ?; yes

1207; Yazza, Ruth; ?-1930; 1 yr; f; yes; F; ?; yes

1234; Hosteen Begay Ah Jinny; 7-11-1930; 81 yr; m; yes; F; ?; yes

DEATHS, (Occurring between April 1, 1930, and March 31, 1931)

KEY: Number on 1930 Census Roll; Name; Date of Death; Age at Death; Sex; Tribe (Navajo, unless otherwise indicated); Ward [yes or no]; Degree of Blood; Cause of Death (if given); At jurisdiction where enrolled [yes or no]; (If "no", where?).

1255; Zonni; 3-1931; 3 yr; f; yes; F; ?; yes

1276; Sonni; ?-1930-31; 17 yr; f; yes; F; ?; yes

1279; Zoni Kay Jenny, Susie Hazel; ?-1930-31; 1 yr; f; yes; F; ?; yes

1515; Ya Des; 5-30-1930; 1 yr; m; yes; F; ?; yes

1525; Knox, Robert; 9-1-1930; 26 yr; m; yes; F; ?; yes

1552; Na Clah Ye He Gee, Billy; 5-19-1930; 24 yr; m; yes; F; ?; yes

1718; Nez, Prudence; 9-3-1930; 15 yr; f; yes; F; ?; yes

1794; Socie; 7-10-1930; 4 yr; f; yes; F; ?; yes

1806; Clizzy Clanni; 1-1931; 96 yr; m; yes; F; ?; yes

1824; Ah Kee Bah, Ruth; 2-1931; 16 yr; f; yes; F; ?; yes

1951; Bizah Haloni's Wife; 7-8-1930; 41 yr; f; yes; F; ?; yes

2297; Na Ta Ne Baloni; 1-1931; 33 yr; m; yes; F; ?; yes

2328; Chl Cow Benna; ?-1930; 37 yr; f; yes; F; ?; yes

2604; Gee Shon; ?-1930; 1 yr; f; yes; F; ?; yes

SUPPLEMENTAL DEATH REPORT

KEY: Name; Date of Death; Age at Death; Sex; Tribe (Navajo, unless otherwise indicated); Degree of Blood; Cause of Death (if given); At jurisdiction where enrolled [yes or no]; (If "no", where?); Residence or Place of Death. [Death certificates not located on Death Rolls.]

(NOTE: No census year or number was given on this report.)

[Mother's name is Bah], Charlotte; 4-5-1928; 1 mo; f; F; Septicemia; yes; Navajo Co, Keams Canyon Hopi Hosp, AZ

Ta Betsy Hosteen; 6-23-1928; 40; f; F; Eclampsia; yes; Navajo Co, Keams Canyon, AZ, [Hosp]

Dejols, Mary Dine; 2-27-1929; 6; f; F; Septicemia; yes; Navajo Co, Keams Canyon, AZ, [Hosp]

Dashee, Julia A; 5-24-1929; 27; f; F; Struck by lightning; yes; Navajo Co, Steamboat Canyon, AZ

Belin Hoani Bay Aszan; ?-1930; 71; f; F; Unknown; yes; Navajo Co, Keams Canyon, AZ, [Not hosp]

Hosteen Ahs Tale; ?-1930; 71; m; F; Unknown; yes; Navajo Co, Keams Canyon, AZ, [Not hosp]

Elliott #479; ?-1930; 25; m; F; Unknown; yes; Navajo Co, Keams Canyon, AZ, [Not hosp]

Elliott, Mrs #480; ?-1930; 18; f; F; Unknown; yes; Navajo Co, Keams Canyon, AZ, [Not hosp]

John #5798; ?-1930; 1; m; F; Unknown; yes; Navajo Co, Keams Canyon, AZ, [Not hosp]

Hosteen Beda Ah Clanny; ?-1930; 80; m; F; Unknown; yes; Navajo Co, Keams Canyon, AZ, [Not hosp]

Be Za De [Wife]; ?-1930; 22; f; F; Unknown; yes; Navajo Co, Keams Canyon, AZ, [Not hosp]

Red Horse, Mark; 11-14-1930; Schoolboy; F; Exposure & starvation; yes; Navajo Co, Hopi Res, AZ

Bitsili, Marie; 5-4-1930; 10; f; F; Bronchopneumonia; yes; Navajo Co, Keams Canyon, AZ

Ashishi, Lunn; 4-29-1930; 7; m; F; Dilatation of heart; yes; Navajo Co, Keams Canyon, AZ

Kinyiannidal, Percy; 12-24-1929; 9; m; F; TB of lungs; no; Ft. Defiance, AZ

Index

A Lah Socie 42
Acade Chene 6
Ace N Terherte 1
Aching Leg 1
Aching Leg's Daughter 20
Ad Ade Se He 20
Ad Ade So He 14
Ad Ade Soc 58
Ad Ade Socie 48
Ad Aye Ah Si Violet Simpson 52
Ad De Chonnie 20
Ad Etch Bahhe 51
Ad Swe See Hoskie 44
Ada 27
Ada Kai 43,59
Ada Soice 47
Aday Chee 44
Aday Tazza 44
Ade Ade Sahe Benna 14
Ade Bagge 56
Ade Bahhe 56
Ah 21
Ah A She Bitse, Hosteen 1
Ah A She, Hosteen 1
Ah A She, Hosteen, Wife 1
Ah Ada Soi 46
Ah Ade 1,7,13,16,44
Ah Ade Bahhe 1,8,14
Ah Ade Chee 46
Ah Ade Chee He 44
Ah Ade Chone 39
Ah Ade Nez 14
Ah Ade Nezzie 14
Ah Ade Si He 3
Ah Ade Socie 4,11
Ah Ade Soe He 33
Ah Ade Soi 1,3,17
Ah Ade Soi Bema 17
Ah Ade Soi, Betty Gambler 2
Ah Ade Yazza 53
Ah Ade Yazze 58
Ah Adie 28
Ah Ana Bah 55
Ah Aye Baahe 24
Ah Aye Ke 21
Ah Aye Yazze 17,32
Ah Ba Bah 43

Ah Bae 27,62
Ah Bay, Wilson Archie 17
Ah Be Chi, Melvin 59
Ah Can Li 1
Ah Can Li's Wife 1
Ah Cane Lee 2
Ah Cayne Bah 25
Ah Che Ne Ne Bah 57
Ah Chee 3
Ah Chee Bah Ho Zoni 29
Ah Chee, Aszan 2
Ah Chi Bitsoni 2
Ah Chole He Cripped, Aszan 2
Ah De 6
Ah De Bay Aszan 3
Ah De Cay 22
Ah De Chi 2,53
Ah De Chi Nez 3
Ah De Chi Nez Bitse 6
Ah De Chi Nez'l Wife 3
Ah De Chi Socie 3
Ah De Chi Socie Bay Aszan 3
Ah De Chi Socie Bedonni 3
Ah De Chi Socie Bedonni's Wife 3
Ah De Chi Socie Bitsie 24
Ah De Chi Yazze 3
Ah De Chi Yazze Bezah Ah 3
Ah De Chi, Lorenzo 61
Ah De Chie 3
Ah De Chi's Wife 2
Ah Deele, Aszan, Martin 4
Ah Deeley, Aszan 4
Ah Di Aye Yazza 3
Ah Di Aye Yazza Benna 3
Ah Ehe Hoskie 45
Ah Gee Bah 62
Ah Gee Kee, Jacob 53
Ah Ha Gee Bah 31
Ah Has Bah 9
Ah Hayne Bah 50
Ah He 39
Ah He De Bah 2,38,55
Ah He Ne Bah 18
Ah Hes De Bah 44
Ah Ho En Tille 4
Ah Hosk Be Ade He 3
Ah Hosteen 4

Index

Ah Kee..38,41	Ahs She, Aszan 5
Ah Kee Bah, Ruth..................................... 68	Ahs Tale Bega, Hosteen 6
Ah Kee Da Bah 25	Ahs Tale Bitsoni, Hosteen.........................6
Ah Na Bah 41,54	Ahs Tale, Hosteen, Aszan 5
Ah Na Des Bah 10	Ahtaye, Hosteen 5
Ah Pade Yazza 31	Ak Ad So Bega..16
Ah Sa Has Bah... 54	Akke Nez Benna.....................................14
Ah See See's daughter 4	Al Di De Bah.....................................20,64
Ah Sha He 23	Al Ka They Bah......................................44
Ah She Badoni #1...................................... 5	Al Na Ha Ge Be 23
Ah She De Bah 2,8	Al Sie He 66
Ah She He 5	Albert 45
Ah She He Bega 5	Ald Zith Si Ho..33
Ah She He Socie....................................... 5	Alice 24
Ah She He's Wife 5	Andrews, George....................................32
Ah Shene Bega 5	Anna 2
Ah Shene Bega's Wife #1 5	Apache 6
Ah Shene Bega's Wife #2 5	Apache, Sylvia 6
Ah Si He 1,3	Arlie 4
Ah So Na De Bah 50	As He De Bah...31
Ah Socie 13	As Hi He Kee 35
Ah Soi E Bah... 10	As Soie Bah..22
Ah Soi Ne Gees Bah 40	As Zan Clock Begay.................................7
Ah Ta De Bah.. 45	Asafee Bah..55
Ah Tad Holani 5	Asch Lee...10
Ah Tade 19	Aschan Begay...37
Ah Tade Chee 42	Asche Bay 6
Ah Tade Na Sarde 5	Asche He 6
Ah Tade Socie 1	Aschee's Wife #2.....................................6
Ah Tade Toll 26	Asdanab Bah, Hilda................................38
Ah Tade Yazza 3,42,43,47	Ash Cuy, White Girl...............................18
Ah Tahe Bahhe, Alice 29	Ash He 4
Ah Toan Sui... 10	Ash Ke De Bah.......................................38
Ah Way 38	Ash Kee Bahhe.......................................33
Ah Yo Nezzie, Aszan 6	Ash She He Socie.....................................7
Ah, Aszan 1	Ash Socie Bah, Priscilla.........................44
Aha De Ah She He 5	Ashe Badoni #2..6
Aha Has Bah......................................36,59	Ashe He, Aszan 7
Aha Na O To 52	Ashe She He 7
Aha Naz Bah 51	Ashe She He Bay Aszan..........................7
Aha Yazza 18	Ashishi, Lunn 69
Ahade 39	Asjans Tou 7
Ahade Soice... 63	Aske 33
Ahs Ah Bah 55	Aske Nez 14
Ahs Has Bah 8	Askie 27
Ahs Na Gees Bah...................................... 6	Asl He, Joe 6
Ahs Nah Bah 45	Asoise De Bah..9

Index

Asta Tes Bah Connie 10
Astzan, Dale 7
Asza Nez.. 43
Aszan 27,32,46,54
Aszan Ah Deele's Wife........................... 4
Aszan Ah Si He 17
Aszan Bah... 57
Aszan Bahhe..........................6,13,35,53
Aszan Bahhe Wife #2 4
Aszan Be Toe Ne................................. 40
Aszan Buy 50
Aszan Chee..............................33,43,59
Aszan Chee Le....................................... 9
Aszan Chee Yazze 6
Aszan Choola 45
Aszan Cispe... 6
Aszan Clizzy.. 28
Aszan Clock Begay Ah......................... 7
Aszan Coy 56
Aszan De Odie.................................... 35
Aszan De Tomne 10
Aszan Deel 12,13
Aszan Gay 23
Aszan Gle He...................................... 14
Aszan Guy 41
Aszan Ha Nu Chary............................. 52
Aszan Has Len.................................... 57
Aszan Kai 48
Aszan Le Zinney................................. 27
Aszan Nez......... 9,14,16,27,37,53,54,66,67
Aszan Sanne Toe He........................... 32
Aszan Schene 50
Aszan Se He 18
Aszan Si He 3
Aszan Sihe 54
Aszan Sipe.. 61
Aszan Socie 4,16,22,26,27,39,44,47,50
Aszan Socie Benna 47
Aszan Socie, Betty................................ 9
Aszan Soi 24,37,42
Aszan Soi Benna 42
Aszan Sone 14
Aszan Ta Ne Zahne 27
Aszan Tahhe 58
Aszan To Ad Lena 8
Aszan Toe Honani 4
Aszan Toede Chonne.......................... 37

Aszan Tot Soi Ne 5
Aszan Whoola 6
Aszan Yazza...........................35,36,44
Aszan Yazze................3,34,36,46,58
Aszan Ye Glo He.................................30
Aszan Yessie 16
Aszan Yo In Title 42
Aszan Zinny 43
Aszan Zon 30
Aszan, Pearl.......................................41
Aszan, Soi 10
Aszanne Ade Aga 25
Aszaynnie 19
Aszonie..3
Atah Ate De.......................................38
Ath Ne Bah..59
Athsecth 40
Athsecth Benna 40
Away Bega 14
Away Yazze 53
Away Yazze Bema 53
Away Yazzie 65
Ay Ah Bah...7
Aye Yaz..49
Aye Yazze 28
Ayede 32
Ayne Bah...9
Az He 10

B Sam..8
Ba Socie 33
Badona, Ray......................................39
Badoni Be Nally 8
Badoni Begay 8
Badoni Bitsi.......................................15
Badoni, Jim 8
Bah 1,4,5,7,8,9,12,13,15,17,22,25,
27,29,31,33,36,37,41,45,51,52,53,55,57,
58,67,69
Bah Ah Cia Hinges Bah 37
Bah Ah Yia Bah 37
Bah Bema..22
Bah Bena Yellow Hair's Wife 19
Bah Chenna 56
Bah Dah De 2
Bah Des Wood 41
Bah Gee...45

73

Index

Bah Ha 29
Bah He 32
Bah He, Johnnie 9
Bah Ho Zone 9
Bah Ho Zonnie 9
Bah Ho Zonnie Bay Aszan 9
Bah Keane 45
Bah Ki So 23
Bah Na Gus 19
Bah Nah 21
Bah Nal De Bah 36
Bah Ne 4
Bah Ne Bah 1
Bah Ne Yah 14
Bah Si He 34
Bah Soi 33
Bah Wanah 9
Bah Yazza 36
Bah Yazze 1,8,51
Bah Ye De 43
Bah Ye Gee Bah 50
Bah Ye Ne 30
Bah Ye Nie 21
Bah Yeth Ne 17
Bahas Zan 26
Bahha 54
Bahha, Hevelle 21
Bahhe 2,3,11,13,23,28,39,43,44,46, 47,50,51,54
Bahhe Ad Ade 6
Bahhe Ah Ade 30
Bahhe Aszan 58
Bahhe Athle 35
Bahhe Badoni 9
Bahhe Na Zoing 29,62
Bahhe She 35
Bahhe Yazze 54
Bahhe, Ada 27,34,61,64,65
Bahhe, Charley 22
Bahhe, Hosteen 11,34
Bahhe, Roy 52,62,66
Bahhe, Susie 49
Bahhee Aszan 37
Bahn Ne Bah 34
Bahs Ne Wah 24
Baish, Hosteen 9
Baj 54

Banna Soi 25
Barney 10
Bash Ne De Ne 10
Baszan Yazze 60
Baw, John 10
Bay Ah De La He 23
Bay Ah La 22
Bay Aszan 49
Bay Aszan Toney 47
Bay De Lahe Bega 10
Bay Gach Be Aye Be 10
Bay Ne Bah 51
Bay Yazzie 9,61
Bays De Bah 37
Be Ah Kee 48
Be Aye De Chizzy Benna 10
Be Aye De Clizzy 10
Be Cak Zi Bah 65
Be Da Ah Thanny Bega, Hosteen 10
Be Do Ne Aszan 11
Be Ga, Hosteen 11
Be Gande Ne, Hosteen 12
Be Gande Ne's, Hosteen, Wife 12
Be Gees, Hosteen 12
Be Gelly 12
Be Goody #2, John 13
Be Goody, David 13
Be Goody, John 13
Be Goody's Wife, John 13
Be Ho Zone Ne 28
Be La Ah Goody 6
Be Lee Na Ge 13
Be Lee Na Ge's Wife 13
Be Lin Je Zinney Benna 13
Be Lon Bega 13
Be Na Le Bahhe, Hosteen 14
Be Na Te He 14
Be Na Te He's Wife 14
Be Sa Va Clanny Bega, Hosteen 15
Be Sinny Badoni, Hosteen 15
Be Sinny Hosteen, Bitse 15
Be Tone Socie 15
Be Ya Ye, Hosteen 16
Be Yelle 16
Be Yelle Becla 16
Be Yo Chee Do 16
Be Za De 16

Index

Be Za De [Wife]	69	Beny Nezzie	15
Be Za De Bega #2	55	Bessie	28,40
Be Zhan Ne Dally, Hosteen	16	Bet Nanny Son	8
Be Zit Ben	16	Betoni	15
Beala Gee Bah	22	Betoni's Wife	15
Becay	10	Betty	8
Becay Bekis	10	Betty Smith	63
Becay Bekis' Wife	10	Beza Da Bega	16
Becay's Son-in-Law #1	10	Beza De Bay Aszan	16
Becay's Son-in-Law #2	10	Bezan De Nee Bega, Hosteen	16
Becay's Wife	10	Bidony Sonny	16
Beck, Clifford	33	Big Gambler, Andrew	53
Beda Ba Ne Sazie	11	Big Gambler, Blanche	2
Beda Ba Ne Sazie's Wife	11	Big Gambler, Sam	53
Bedah Vannie Hosteen	11	Big Jim	16
Bee He	27	Big Jim's Wife	16
Bega #1, Charley	12	Big John	17
Bega #2	12	Big John Bitse	22
Bega #2 Wife	67	Big John's Wife	17
Bega De Nege, Hosteen	12	Big Man	17
Bega, Denny	27	Big Pete	17
Begah Ah Jinny's, Hosteen, Wife	12	Billy	7,17,19
Beganepaz Mt Bega	12	Billy Catherine	17
Begay, Harry	37	Billy Pete, Old	17
Begay, Hosteen	12	Billy Wild Bill	4
Begay, Johnnie	11	Billy, Jim	17
Begay, Mark	42	Billy, John	17,27,30
Begay, Tony	11	Billy, Katy	17
Begoody Aszan, John	13	Billy, Mary	17,64
Bejesi Be Yaz	13	Bina Chee	20
Beka, Tony's Wife	11	Bini Key	59
Belin Hoani Bay Aszan	69	Bis Kee	40
Bema Glee Ha Bah	35	Bish Be Toe Badone	18
Ben, James	14	Bit An Ne Aszan #2	18
Ben, Jim	14	Bitiny Goy Hostine	18
Ben, John	14	Bitone Chee	31,62
Ben, Joy	14	Bitse Bahhe, Hosteen	18
Bena Bahhe, Aszan	14	Bitsey Becay's Daughter	18
Bena The Be	16	Bitsey Begay's Daughter, Jane	61
Benna	21	Bitsi	8
Benna, Eddie	14	Bitsi Goody	18
Benna, Edward	50	Bitsi, Sarh	52
Benna, Hosteen	14	Bitsie Bitsoni Zahshe He	35
Benna, Ken	15	Bitsie Le Bahhe Bega, Hosteen	18
Benna's, Hosteen, Wife	14	Bitsie Le Bahhe Bega's, Hosteen Wife	18
Benny	4,15	Bitsie Le Bahhe, Aszan	18
Benoto He Bena	14	Bitsili, Marie	69

Index

Bitsoni 39	Cay Bean De 22
Bitsoni Bahhe 35	Cay Cans Bah 40
Bitsoni Hosteen An Asis 18	Cay Na Yah 2
Bitsoni Slice, Erick 35	Cay Ne Bah 34
Bitsoni Yellow Horse 19	Cay Wood 59
Bitsy Bitsoci Badoni 19	Cay Wood Benna 59
Bitsy Bitsoci's Wife 19	Cesoar Selago 16
Bitsy Bitsoni Sonne 19	Ch Le Bahhe Bitsone 24
Bizah Haloni 19,24	Ch Skizzy Bega 25
Bizah Haloni, Hosteen 19	Cha Hay Thompson, Charley 22
Bizah Haloni's Wife 68	Cha He Bega 22
Bizante 12	Chans Na Bah 42
Black Horse 19	Charley 1,55
Black Man's Son 19	Charley John 22
Black Mans' Son, Billy 64	Charley Watchman 63
Black Mustache 20	Charley, Dorothy 8
Black Mustache's Wife 20	Charley, Lucy 23
Black Sheep, Annie 20	Charley, Sam 23
Black Sheep, Woody 20	Charlie 23,49
Black Sheep's Wife 20	Charlie B 37
Black, Anna 20	Charlotte 69
Blacksheep 67	Che Ha Bah 41
Blind Woman 20	Che The Chize Ne 23
Blue Lake's Son 20	Chee 2,6,7,18,30,31,32,47,50,53,67
Boots 20	Chee Bahhe 9,64
Botsio Gpu Bega 18	Chee Barn 39
Boy Aszan 45	Chee Cay 23
Bridge, John 20	Chee Cay Bega 23
Bruce 30	Chee Cay's Wife 23
Bryant 15	Chee Chee 5
Bucking Horse's Mother 20	Chee Dena Begay 19
Bucking Horse's Son 20	Chee He Hoskie 11
Burt 20	Chee Hosteen 37
	Chee Kan 13
Can 1,24,61	Chee Kee 48
Cardy Bah 45	Chee Nadah 30
Carl 21	Chee Ne 46
Cash Goulie 21	Chee Ne Dah 13
Cash Goulie Bega 21	Chee Ne, George 27
Cash Goulie's Daughter 21	Chee Nez 56
Cash Goulie's Wife 21	Chee Ye Yazza 50
Cash Gro Lie Bega 21	Chee Ye Ye 26
Cash Grolie Bega #4 21	Chee Ye, Ethel 59
Cash Grolie Begay's Wife #2 21	Chee Zin Bin Ne 44
Casper 15	Chee Zini, Hosteen 23
Catholic 25	Chee, Aszan 23
Caw, Jane 20	Chee, Augusta 27

Index

Chee, Waldine	45	Claude	36
Cheesee Ana's Wife	23	Claw, Gordon	8
Cheesee Na Ana Bega	23	Clay Chi Be Ash Dog Bitten	42
Cheesee Nanna Bega #2	23	Clay Yazze	26
Chelley Bema	57	Clay, Hosteen	26
Chelly	48	Cle Bah	27
Chen Has Bah, Emma	22	Cle Bitsey	26
Cher Ken	33	Cle Chee Beds, Hosteen	27
Chet Chilli Yet Toe, Hosteen	24	Cle Ha Bah	27
Chi Che Tade Bahhe	13	Cle Ha Bah, Sevina	27
Chilli, Teddy	25	Cle Has Bah	20
Chilly	5	Cle See	39
Chisay Ja He Bitsi	48	Cle Zinny, Hosteen	27
Chizzy Nez Badoni	24	Clee Chee, Hosteen	27
Chizzy Nez Bitsi	24	Cleo	28
Chizzy Ua Billy	24	Clesn Yazze	55
Chizzy Ua Billy's Wife	24	Cli Ahs Na Bah	57
Chizzy Uah Billy Badoni	24	Clie Na Ne Bah	8
Chizzy's Daughter	24	Clie Ne Bah	55
Chl Cow Benna	68	Clizzie Thane	27
Chlesh	20	Clizzie Thane's Wife	27
Cho Ho	39	Clizzy	27,35
Cho Li	10,42	Clizzy Clanni	68
Chonne	13	Clizzy Clanny	28
Chonne, Roger	13	Clizzy Clanny Bay Aszan	28
Chonnie	55,59	Clizzy Clanny, Aszan	28
Chosie Ci Benna	24	Clizzy De Seayye Goat Skins	27
Chosie Si	24	Clizzy Klanny, Joe	28
Chus Chee	11	Clizzy Tanne, Hosteen	28
Cis See	44	Clony Zanni, Bessie	62
Cisco	25	Clony Zanni, Elsie	62
Cisco's Wife	25	Clony Zinni	28
Cisse Nez Bega	25	Closi, Hosteen	29
Cisse Zan	25	Closi's, Hosteen, Wife	29
Clah	3,6,25,46	Cloth Be Nelly #2, Aszan	29
Clah Ah Ne Ne	26	Con Soi Hosh	29
Clah Bahhe	13	Cook, Jim	29
Clah Klinny	26	Cook, John	29,30
Clah Soi Bitsi	55	Cora	2,12
Clah Yazza	26	Cow Boy	29
Clah, Aszan	25	Cow Boy's Wife	29
Clah, James	25	Cowboy's Sister	30
Clah, John King	25	Crokekd Finger's Wife	30
Clah's Son	26	Crokked Finger	30
Clah's Son's Wife	26	Crooked Finger's Daughter #3	32
Clanny Zinny Begay	26	Crooked Finger's Grand-son	30
Clark, Robert	15		

Index

Da Be Bah	40
Da Bitsoni Goody	30
Da Bitsoni Goody's Wife	30
Da Cee	27
Da Da Ha Doody	11
Da Has Bah	31
Da Kai	47
Da La Nezzie	31
Da Nas Bah	15
Da Va Chee	31
Da Va He	32
Da Va Socie	32
Da Va Socie's Wife	32
Da Yazzie	24
Da Yezzzie	61
Dade Wood Hoskie	56
Daf Ah She No	30
Daffy, Mike	31
Dah Ad Zin	1
Dah Ah She Ne's Wife	30
Dah Ak Nis Sisi	36
Dah De Bah	55
Dah He	22
Dah La Chee Benna	2
Dah La Than Ne	31
Dah Na Bah	40
Dah Nah Bah	59
Dah She Bah	8
Dah Ton Ha	54
Dah Yous	4
Dale	4
Dallas Eschon	53
Dan	11,31
Dan #3	38
Dan #4	38
Dan Yazza's Wife	31
Daniel	23
Das Wood	8
Dase, Aszan	31
Dashee, Julia A	69
Dashene, Lottie	18
Datenany, Norton	41
Datenany, Susie	41
Datenany, Violet	41
David	12
Dayate, She Bega She	32
De Cho Li	32
De Cho Li Bema Hosteen	32
De Da Wood Hoskie Benna	56
De Jole	32
De Joly Denna	33
De Joly Denna's Wife	33
De Len Se Jinny	33
De Na La Cui	33
De Na La Gui's Wife	33
De Na Sea Nava He	34
De Na So Denny	33
De Na Soi, Alvin	27
De Nah Ah Daye	21
De Ne Sea Nava He's Wife	34
De Net De Cho Li	23
De Sho	16
De Si	34
De Wazza Bitse	26
De Wizzie Bega	36
De Wozzie	36
De Ye Te	38
De Ye Te's Wife	38
De Zah He	38
Dead Horse	32
Deel Begay #3, Hosteen	32
Deel Begay, Hosteen	32
Deel Begay, Hosteen, Wife	32
Deel Hoskie	5
Deel, Hosteen	32
Dejols, Mary Dine	69
Dema Ach He	65
Dena	41
Dena Ah Ne	33
Dena Ah Si	33
Dena Chee	55
Dena Chilli Be Kis	33
Dena De Jole Begay, Mose	33
Dena La Guy	34
Dena La Guy's Wife	34
Dena Le Guy Begay	34
Dena Nes Bah	34
Dena Si He	7
Dena Sihe	35
Dena Socie	12
Dena Socie Bega	34
Dena Socie, Richard	54
Dena Socie, Ross	19
Dena Soi	2,35,64

Index

Dena Sosie.. 67	Detcelia 36
Dena Yazze, David 8	Dewey 31
Dena, Fred 48	Diana 11
Dene Socie... 13	Dick...21,28,46,56
Dene Ye Wood Benna 34	Dina Ani Bega......................................36
Denet Asoises 34	Dina Yazza...24
Denet Bahhe 35,43,57,59	Dineyazhe, Phillips..............................37
Denet Bahhe Bema 43	Dinneyazhe, Allen 37
Denet Chee 44	Dinny..37
Denet Da Chee..................................... 35	Diny Azhe 37
Denet Le Chee Detchon....................... 37	Dis Bah..6,29
Denet Nemore...................................... 11	Dis Bah, Mary Brown 17
Denet Socie Bega 35	Dis Goody 17
Denet Soi 14	Dis Wood 24
Denet Toli 50	Do Ah De Si He, Hosteen....................37
Denet Tolie.. 3	Do Choenny 37
Denna Ach He 36,64	Do Ha Bah..67
Denna Bah He 34	Do Ha He, Hosteen..............................37
Denna Bahhe 6,42	Do Ha Tahhe's Wife 37
Denna Be Yazzie 14	Do Has Tahhe......................................37
Denna Chee 62	Do Lee Ho Zonie..................................37
Denna Guo... 35	Do So He 19
Denna Guo's Wife................................ 35	Do Yazze..27,51
Denna Guy......................................22,61	Do Ye Te Hostine.................................38
Denna Kai.......................................14,61	Do Ye Te Hostine's Wife......................38
Denna Nez 34	Dobah Askie...37
Denna She Bahhe 11	Dolea 30
Denna Socie 23	Donald..34,47
Denna Soi 53	Dorothy 8
Denna Yazza.................................8,9,53	Du Yah 13
Denna Yazze.. 54	Duna Ne Mozzie..............................11,64
Dennea Sini Cate He........................... 62	
Dennea Sini Gate He 31	E He..59
Dennet Bahhe, Pedro 31	Earl...2
Dennet She Ne Gah 31	Edgar..15
Dennie Socie.. 9	Edgar Miller..28
Dennis..13,59	Edith...22
Dennit Chee 2	Edna...46
Denoc Ah She He 35	Edward, Archie....................................50
Denoc, Harry 35	Eityantso, Sarah..................................12
Des Bah 8,19,36	Eli..24
Des Dah Ade 56	Elizabeth..19
Des Wood 36	Elizibel...38
Des Yah Toni Bega 36	Elliott #479..69
Desbah..35,36	Elliott, Mrs #480 69
Deswood Hoskie................................... 38	Elmer...19,24
Desyah Tone 36	Elsie...28,44

Index

Emil	34
Emma	21,57
Emory	40
Ernest	55
Eschee	38
Eschee's Son	38
Esky, Mike	56
Esquela Bega #8	38
Esquela Begga #7	4
Ess Nezzie	49
Esta	38
Esta Na	38
Ethel	26,54
Etoity Yazza	38
Etoity Yazza Bay Aszan	38
Etsidy	16,39,47
Etsidy Bega	39
Etsidy;s Daughter	39
Etsidy's Wife	39
Etsitty Son	39
Etsitty's Son's Wife	39
Etta	3
Felix	15
Fhe Wah He	39
Florence	8
Frank	26,39,40
Frank Small	5
Frank, Jack	40
Frank, May	62
Frank, Milton	40
Frank, Tom	40
Frank, Wife Of Charley	40
Frank's Wife	67
Fred	49
Gana Bay Aszan, Old Hosteen	40
Gana, Jack	40
Gath	12,59
Gath Li	59
Gee	23,39,59
Gee Hal Bitsey	30
Gee Shon	68
Gee Toli Octavia Nez	55
Gee Tolli	10
Gee Zine	51
Gee Zinni	65
Gee, Claire	40
Gee, Guy	40
Geene, Gus	36
Gemmie, Old Hosteen	40
Gene	40
Gene Be Nelly, Eddie	41
Gene Benally Hosteen	40
Gene Gega, Hosteen	41
Gene Ne Ho, Hosteen	41
George	41,63
George, John	41
Geprge	56
Gertrude Jashivenka	63
Gis Chone De	63
Gle Des Bah	23
Gle Ha Bah	17
Glee Ha Bah	15
Glee Has Bah	36
Glenie Bah	32
Glenn	7,45,46
Gli Ha Bah	41
Glic Yazza	25
Goth	15
Goth Bema	15
Gray Hat's Grandson, Bessie	65
Gucy, Robert	2
Gulic Nah	54
Guy	7,28,35,37,46
Guy Aye Soi	39
Guy He	15
Guy John Gold	3
Guy Le	36
Guy Socie	39
Guy Yazze	42
Guy Zannie, Emma	49
Gyye	7
Ha Cha Yazze	40
Ha De Bah	56
Ha Gees Bah	14
Ha Goes Bah Denna	14
Ha Ha Gleen	43
Ha Na Ne Bah	9
Ha Wood Hoskie	2
Hacke Bahhe	53
Hade, Charley	36
Haloni Beda, Paul	62

Index

Hanesbay	36
Hanibah	36
Hardy, David	28
Hardy, Guy	28
Harold	2
Harrison	31
Harry	17,26,29
Has Bah	24,31,47
Has Bah Tsitnot Jinnie	59,66
Has Ne Hean	55
Has Nes Bah	60
Has Nez Bah	21
Has Wood	15
Has Zani	27
Haske Haswood	15,61
Hazel	25
He De Cho Le	17
He Dog Wood	19
He Nic Aye, Benjamin	46
Helen	52
Helen Small	4
Herman	5,63
Hily	7
Hitulia Deyanawood	18
Ho Che Yazzie	62
Holkie Si Hah Zah	34
Hollywood, Mark	31
Homer	26
Hon Yazze	19
Hos Che Yazzie	40
Hosh Con Bitsi	1,13
Hosk Aschee	6
Hosk Con Bitsey	57
Hosk Ni Con	64
Hosk Ni Yap	65
Hosk The Ne Yah	26,61
Hosk Yel He Wad	45
Hoska Nae Wood	43
Hoske Bahhe	66
Hoske Newood, Joe	38
Hoske Tahe	66
Hoskee Yazzie	64
Hoski Theda	4
Hoskie	22,31,33,39,48,63,64
Hoskie Ah Si He	20
Hoskie Asocie	44
Hoskie Bahhe	6,13,23,31,48,51,57
Hoskie Bahhe Benna	57
Hoskie Beel	35,62
Hoskie Buy	28
Hoskie Chee He	44
Hoskie Dah He Ya	50
Hoskie De Wood, Otho	43
Hoskie Ha Ye Zen Bit Sui	28
Hoskie He Li Wood	34
Hoskie Kee Nas Wood	60
Hoskie Na Aye Da Yah	15
Hoskie Na Da	52
Hoskie Na Das	52
Hoskie Na Hele	34
Hoskie Na Thel	12
Hoskie Na Ya	1
Hoskie Na Yah	20
Hoskie Nas Woody	51
Hoskie Ne Ha Wood	5
Hoskie Ne She Ye	7
Hoskie Ne She Ye, King	64
Hoskie Ne Tee	41
Hoskie Nez	26
Hoskie Si Si	7
Hoskie Sile	5,64
Hoskie Socie	9
Hoskie Soi	47
Hoskie Soi Bena	47
Hoskie Ta Des Wood, Raymond	60
Hoskie Tahe	47
Hoskie Tas Wood	47
Hoskie Tole	37
Hoskie Toli	49
Hoskie Woody	34
Hoskie Ya Nan To	52
Hoskie Ya Ne Ya	1
Hoskie Yah Nah Zah	34
Hoskie Yath Ha Da	6
Hoskie Yazza	19,54
Hoskie Yazze	66
Hoskie Yazzie	11
Hoskie Ye Da Ni Ya	1
Hoskie Ye Na Soi	15
Hoskie Yo Ga	17
Hoskie Zohnne	6
Hosteen	55
Hosteen Ah She Bitse	51
Hosteen Ah Tale	69

Index

Hosteen Be Da Ah Clanny	28	Jinney Toe Honani	46
Hosteen Be Za	63	Jinny Schon	30
Hosteen Beda Ah Clanny	69	Jo Le La, Helen	21
Hosteen Begay Ah Jinny	67	Joe	58
Hosteen Blind's Daughter	21	Joel	12,46
Hosteen Chee Be Beda	9	John #5798	69
Hosteen Chee Bema	8	John Nez Clanny Bitsi	1
Hosteen Cle Chee	57	John, Jr	50
Hosteen Clizzy Thane's Wife	28	Johnnie	20,30,44
Hosteen Deel	24	Jola	21
Hosteen Gana Bitse #2	40	Juanita	7
Hosteen Gann Bitse #1	24	Julia	46
Hosteen Gene	16	Julian	57
Hosteen Guy	54		
Hosteen Na Ha Ah	2	Kahn	38
Hosteen Nez Day Aszan	39	Kai, Ada	29
Hosteen Schene Bitse #1	26	Kan	29,50
Hosteen Socie Yazzie	19,64	Kan Bahhe	43
Hosteen Soi Bitsie	42	Kan Soie	43,66
Hosteen Yazza	53	Katherine	15
Hosteen Yazza Bay Aszan	52	Ke Ha Ne Bah	12
Hosteen Yazza's Wife	53	Ke To Shia Bitsoni	35
Hosteen Yazze, Abraham	33	Ked Niche	28
Hosteen Yo En Tilli	67	Kee	4,6,7,11,16,21,26,27,45,47,49,54
Hostine Bega	38	Kee Ah Si Ne	32
Hostine Nez	38	Kee An Na Si He	59
Howard	34	Kee Ath Ye	26
Hunter, Harry	2	Kee Bah He	12
		Kee Bahhe	4,13,18,25,35,36,57,60
Ione	22	Kee Buy	33
Irene	40	Kee Chee	14,34,35,42,49,59,61
Irene Nelson	63	Kee Da Soui	59
Isda, Lorenzo	53	Kee Ha Das Bah, Ada	31
Izzy Niez Bega, Joe	65	Kee Kai	53,66
		Kee Lay	12
Ja Nas Bah	25	Kee Ne Chonie	50
Jack	8,40	Kee Nez	37
Jackson, Anita	26	Kee On Nez	2
Jah Te	1	Kee Ony Nez Be Nally	17
Jah Ye	24	Kee Se Ne	59
James, Benjamin	51	Kee Si He	25
Jane	18	Kee Socie	39,52
Jean	14	Kee Socie Brown, Paul	6
Jennie	29,54	Kee Soi	5,11,13,49,55,61
Jimmy	49	Kee Soise He	3,64
Jim's Wife	29	Kee Sone	35
Jina Bah	47	Kee Toli	50

Index

Kee Tolle 23	Lona Zon Bitsi 31
Kee Tso 52	Lorene 57
Kee Yazza 36,42,47,56,60	Lorenzo 2,21
Kee Yazze 26,45,49	Lorenzo Smith 36
Kee Yazze, Norman 13	Lottie 56
Kee Yazzie 4,10	Louise 50
Keeho Benna 18	Lucille 30
Keh 20	Lucy 40
Ken 33,44	Luella 15
Ken Ah Sis 3	Luke 31
Ken He Bah 48	
Ken Tazza 39	Mabel 10,38
Ken Yazza 37	Mahaz 29
Ken Yazz's Mother 19	Mahme 25
Ken, Ken 3	Marie 28
Keni 4	Marion 56
Keni Hez Beh 4	Mark 19
Kenneth 37	Martha 56
Ket Ce Lia #1 Wife 36	Mary 37,40
Ket Ce Lia Wife #2 36	Mary Ellen 28
Kin Yazze 4	Maxwell 23
Kina Big Gamber 53	May 39,56,57
King 7	Melvin 12
Kinyiannidal, Percy 69	Minnie 30,60
Kirk, Charles 51	Morgan, Clinton 31
Kirkton, Leo 51	Morgan, Dan 31
Kishony, Lee 6	Morris 41,53
Knox 44	Mose N Terperte 1
Knox, Robert 68	Mose's Wife 10
Krr Socie 22	Mozzie 41
	Muzzie 21
La Ne Zinne 63	
Lat, Bessie 62	Na 39
Laura 47	Na Ah Ziaay 20
Lavo, John 17,64	Na Ah Zizzie 2
Lawrence 5	Na Bah 9
Leawah Big Gambler 53	Na Bleen Has Bah 34
Lettie 14	Na Chi Chee 28
Lewis, Charley 65	Na Chi De He Yea Aszan 10
Lewis, Jim 65	Na Clah Ye He Gee, Billy 68
Lewis, Laura 65	Na Dach Na De Ya 44
Lewis, Tommy 65	Na Dich Ha Done 37
Li He, Jerry 22	Na Gle Ha Bah 17
Lily 41	Na Glee Ne Bah 43
Little Boy 35	Na Gleen Na Ne Bahhe 13
Lois 26	Na Glen 5,61
Lola 46,59	Na Glen Ta Ne 62

Index

Na Glic Ah Lee De Dah 18
Na La Yezzie 30,62
Na Ma Zec 19
Na Nah Way 12
Na Ne Bah 25
Na Ne Ne He 22
Na Nes Bah 42
Na Nez Bah 12
Na Soi He 27
Na Ta Ne Bah 11
Na Ta Ne Baloni 68
Na Zeln 50
Nad Ads Nad As 17
Nad Ath He Has Bega 11
Naglen 12
Nah 32
Nah Chee 5
Nah Chet 56
Nah Cli 42
Nah Gle Nes Bah 40
Nah Zien 39
Nas Bah 48,59
Nas Cott 47
Nava 9
Ne 57
Ne Azhs 17
Ne Bah 25,51,65
Ne Cay Bah 26
Ne Chonne 57
Ne Gees Bah 59
Ne Glenne Bah 55
Ne Ka Ta Day Wood 53
Ne La Ta Dey Wood, Lorenzo 66
Ne Na Ges Bah 56
Ne Nas Bah 57
Ne Neze 4
Ne Pah Ye Ne Yea 62
Ne Ta Ye Tie 50,66
Ne Te, Hostee 63
Ne The He Wood 1,64
Ne Zi Bah 50
Ned 15,34
Nee He 41
Nee The Bah 1
Nellie 38,52
Nelson, Annie 65
Nelson, Chas 63

Nelson, May 46
Nemore, Dennet 63
Nez 1,28,36
Nez Aszan 44
Nez Clanny Begay, Ross 65
Nez Hosteen 57
Nez, Charley 9
Nez, Howard 7
Nez, Mae 63
Nez, Prudence 68
Nez, Sam 52
Nezzie Hoskie, Dan 20
Ni Glen Ta Ne 35
Ni Na Bah 65
Nic Ge Ha Talye Bitse 16
Nina 56
No Have Zha 59,66
No Soi 30
No Tah 40
Nona 3
Norma 29
Noskie Nad A Ho 11
Nozzie Ad Ade 48

Olch Tihe 30
Oscar 52
Oscine 57
Oth Ta Ye 37
Otho N Poole 17

Paddock, Anthony 32
Pat 21
Paul 50
Pearl Aszan 63
Peck, Snoch 43
Peterson, Farmer 22
Peterson, Gloria 22,61,63
Philip 28
Phoebe 8
Priscilla 17

Ralph 32
Ray 19
Raymond 42
Ray's Brother 39
Red Horse, Mark 69
Red House 4

Index

Richard Long	28
Robinson, Rosilie	65
Roger	28
Rosie ?	63
Roy	19
Ruby	8,17,50
Ruth	7,37,56
Ruth Ann	34
Sa Da Skezen Bay Aszan	21
Sa Ei Bitse	41
Sa Nenah	18
Sa Thli	14
Sah Aye	20
Sah Bah He	18
Salah Bitsi Goody	46
Sallie	11
Sally	8
Salt, Evan	1
Sam	22,29,46
Sam B. Clara	67
Sangster, Sybil	58
Sannie, Charlie	67
Schan	38
Schonnie	39
Scott, Slyvania	11
Se Chee He	29
Se Le Bahhe	53
Se Se Zinna	49
Se See	36
See He	18
See See	58
Seginey Begay	23
Sells Peter	10
Selma	30
Sene Askisi He	3
Sens	3
Sew Bah	22
Sh Le Ne	52
Sh Way	26,61
Shafgy Bema	2
Shati	35
Shay	33
Shay Chilly	2
Shay Way	16
She	46
She Cay Be Jay Bitsi	22

She Cay Benna	23
She Cay Yazze	2
She Chilli, Billy Mike	7
She He	36
Shepherd, Donald	15
Shepherd, Wesley	53
Shonie	53
Si	15
Si Bah Ah Goodie Yazza	6
Si Bahhe	3,22
Si Chee	46
Si Chil Lie	35
Si Chille	52
Si Doth Li Bahhe Hoske De Wood	51
Si He	3,4,14,22,40,41
Si He Bahhe	34
Si Hes Bah	47
Si Licth Bahhe	26
Si Na Jinny	8
Si Si	23,54
Si Soi	13
Si Yah	11
Sice Kee	35
Sie Ye	1
Sihe	21,34,42
Sikan Yellow Horse Jason	51
Silver Hat Band's Wife #2	33
Silversmith Jim's Wife	67
Sisce	28
Sisco Aszan	55
Slah Bitsi	39
Smith, Denna	39
Smith, Enoch	22
Smith, Grace	38
Smith, Henry	41
Smith, Sally	39
Smith, Samuel	22
Smith, Tilman	39
So See	33
Socie	4,6,13,16,20,30,31,33,49,50,68
Socie Clah, Yellow Hair	38
Socie Clizzy Klanny	26
Socie Dennet	45
Socie Wes	30
Socie Yazza	31
Socie Zah Nez	41
Socie, Charley	19

Index

Soe	20
Soe Benna	20
Soh Gro Ve, Betty	11
Soh Gro Ve, Gilford	11
Soha Hoskie	29
Soi	46,57
Soi Aszan Bega	41
Soi Ba Doni, Hosteen	42
Soi Bega Badoni, Hosteen	42
Soi Bega, Hosteen	42
Soi Begay, Eugene	42
Soi Begay, Lorene	42
Soi Begay, Raymond	66
Soi E	4
Soi He	2,25
Soi Yazze	35
Soi Ze	27
Soi, Aszan	41
Soi, Hosteen	42,43
Soi, Hosteen, Wife #1	42
Soi, Hosteen, Wife #2	42
Soie Ahway	33
Soise Bema	23
Solzie	15
Son Sguy Zahn Kay	6
Sone, Hosteen	43
Soni Sotsis, Martha	32
Sonne	35,39
Sonni	68
Sonnie	33
Sonnie Hosteen Yazzie	48
Sophia	45
Soui, Hosteen	43
Stanley	22
Stephen	20
Susie	49
Sylva	7
T Bah He, Aszan	43
Ta Bah Ha De Chi Li Bitsi	34
Ta Bah Ha Socie	17
Ta Bah He Bega	43
Ta Bah He Soue	43
Ta Bah He Soue's Wife	43
Ta Bahhe	15
Ta Betsy Hosteen	69
Ta Chee Ne, Aszan	43

Ta Chene Ha Socie	53
Ta Des Wood	18
Ta Dis Bah, Vera	18
Ta Nah Bah	32
Ta Ne Yah	7
Ta Ne Zah	44
Ta Ni Zane Yazza	44
Ta Ye Soi He, John Scott	44
Tah	44
Tah Bah	43
Tah Bah He Socie Bega	43
Tah Bahhe	43
Tah Des Bah	8
Tah Dis Bah	44
Tah Na Bah	15
Tah Na Ne Guy	44
Tah Ne Bah	49,67
Tah Ne Zane Socie	44
Tah Nezzie Soise	47
Tah Si Ah	3
Tajachine, Bill	36
Tally, Frank	65
Tane Bah Yazzie	14,64
Tanie Sa Ne Yazza	46
Tas Dah	18
Tat Chee Ne	44
Tat Na Zahne Socie	44
Taus Bah	67
Taylor, Howard	55
Te Ne's Wife	45
Tee Ne	45
Than, Willie Kay	21
Thani	2,61
The He	4
They Wood	53
Thick Woman	45
This He Kee	48
Thise Aszan	44
Timothy	57
To Ad Lena, Aszan	45
To Ba Honani Begay	45
To Bah Des Clinny, Herbert	22
To De Chenah Denah	45
To De Chene	45
To Dis Dah Dena	18
To La Son	45
To Li	10

Index

Toe Ah Hanie 45	Way Ah Socie.. 7
Toe Ah Honni Begay 45	Way Bahhe 23,31
Toe Ah Honni Begay's Wife 45	Way Chilly 3
Toe Cle Chene, Hosteen 46	Way Chonz.. 5
Toe De Chee, Aszan 46	Way He 24
Toe De Cheene 55	Way She He 9,30,64
Toe De Chene, Aszan 46	Way She Ne Bahhe............................... 48
Toe De Chenne 46	Way Showie 32
Toe De Cohns, Hosteen 46	Way Si He 26
Toe Honam 46	Way Soi 19,61
Toe Honani Bay Aszan 47	Way Yazza 51
Toe Honani Bitse 47	Way, Aszan, Bayby Woman 48
Toe Honani Hoskie 47	Waya, Emerson 38
Toe Ne 25	Waychee, Winifred 27
Toe Soi Ne Socie 47	Waye Bahhe 12
Toe Soi Ne Socie's Wife 47	We Mozzir Dena Hosteen 48
Toedee Cohns Badoni 46	Wesley... 48
Tolea 18,29,49	Wesley, Charley 48
Tolea Kee 48	White Hair, Ralph 54
Tolea, June... 49	White Line Rock Man 48
Toli 26,42,46	White Man, Albert................................. 44
Toli Bema 46	White Man, Joe 49
Tolie 1,4	White Man, Sam.................................... 49
Tolle 60	White Man's Brother 49
Tollie 8,9,13,61	White Water's Son 49
Tom 47	White, Fanny 42
Tom Joe 47	Whoola 58
Tommy 41	Wide Foot.. 49
Toney... 47	Wide Foot's Son 49
Toode Cheney....................................... 47	Wide Foot's Son's Wife 49
Tso Die 45	Wide Foot's Wife.................................. 49
Tuce... 40	William.. 49
	Willie... 37
Ugashe 47	Willie Begay... 50
Use Chilly 58	Willie, Fred 50
Ush Nes Nezzie, Aszan 48	Willie, John 49,50
Utan Hoskie 48	Willie, May 50
	Wilson 32,63
Wah De Bah 47	Wilson Man... 50
Walter, George 48	Wilson Man's Wife............................... 50
Walthie 23	Wilson, Joe 50
Wana Wood Hoskie.............................. 18	Wilson, John.. 50
Wartz... 48	Wilson, Woodrow 50
Watson, Alfred 48	Wince.. 28
Watson, Amy.. 48	Winker... 51
Watson, Dan 48	Wood.. 38,51
Watson, Don 48	Wood, Yend 63

Index

Woode 45	Yazza Kee 35,54
Woody 4,41,63	Yazza Na Chene 54
Woody, Benjamin 51	Yazza Nachehe Wife #2 54
Worker Bega 51	Yazza Yazza 38
Worker Begay 51	Yazza, Annie 13
Worker Begay's Wife 51	Yazza, Aszan 52
	Yazza, Dicker 52
Ya 8	Yazza, Grace 49
Ya Des 68	Yazza, Harold 26
Ya Des Bah 15	Yazza, Hoarwwn 53
Ya Ha Bah 67	Yazza, Hosteen 53
Ya Na Ani De Yaz 52	Yazza, Howard 54
Ya Na Bah 51,67	Yazza, May 26
Ya Na Ne Bah 51	Yazza, Nettie 43
Ya, Joe 52	Yazza, Roma 29
Yade Dah 17	Yazza, Ruth 67
Yah 49	Yazze 5,20,32,41,55
Yah Be Bahhe 25	Yazze Bega, Hosteen 55
Yah De Bah 46	Yazze To To Gene 55
Yah De Wood 46,52	Yazze Yie Hosteen Bela 44
Yah Na Bah 33	Yazze, Ada 62
Yah Na Byanna 21	Yazze, Aszan 54
Yah Na Ne, Aszan 52	Yazze, Bahhe 54
Yah Nah Bah 15	Yazze, Billy 17
Yah Ne Bah 12,46,48,50,67	Yazze, George 55
Yah Ner Yazze 54	Yazze, Grace 28
Yah She 1	Yazze, Hosteen 55
Yah Si 26	Yazze, Hosteen, Wife 55
Yah Yazze 42	Yazze, Nora 28
Yah Yuh 2	Yazzie 30,56
Yahhe Wood 53	Yazzie Ad Ade 49
Yana Wood 38	Yazzie Away 54
Yazza 1,4,35,42,45,53,58	Yazzie Bahhe 55
Yazza Ach 54	Yazzie De Han Ya 48
Yazza Ada 51	Yazzie Hoskie 24
Yazza Aszan 23	Yazzie Hosteen 56
Yazza Away 57	Yazzie John 64
Yazza Aye 21	Yazzie Kee 7,30
Yazza Bah 31,39	Yazzie Zahn 58
Yazza Begay 52	Yazzie, John 1
Yazza Bitsey, Hosteen 52	Ye Ane Bah 48
Yazza Black Horse 19	Ye Aye Zaht Hoskie 30
Yazza Chene's Wife 54	Ye Bah De Wood Hoskie 18
Yazza De Nez, Jack 30	Ye Cahs 40
Yazza Hoskie 15,18,21,49	Ye Cat Da Su Ze 51
Yazza Hosteen 52	Ye Da He Lo Wood 24
Yazza Hostine 52	Ye Da Hes Bah 24

Index

Ye Da Hes Bema 24
Ye De Bah 52
Ye De Bah, Bessie Rope 29,62
Ye Des Bah 53
Ye Des Wood 53
Ye Dis Bah 52
Ye Gos Bah 22
Ye Ha Bah 40
Ye He Bah 32
Ye Li Wood 29
Ye Na Bah 34
Ye Na Yah 52
Ye Na Yah Benna 52
Ye Ne Ah 26
Ye Ne Bah 51,65
Ye Ne No Da, Andrew 51
Ye Ne Tahe 30
Ye Ne Wood 62
Ye Ne Yaz 24
Ye Ne Ye Bah Way Chee 55
Ye Nes Bah 59
Ye Nez Bah 20,51,57
Ye Ni Bah 51
Ye Seth Hoskie 12
Ye Si Si Bega, Hosteen 52
Ye Soi 2
Ye Sone Bah 15
Ye Ta Ne Bah 44
Ye Tas Bah 24
Ye Wol Die 11
Ye Zunth 2
Yee He Yai 57
Yees Na 57
Yel Ne Bah 23
Yel Ne Kay 13
Yell Wood De 10,61
Yellow Hair 4,56
Yellow Hair, Chester 19
Yellow Hair, Esther 19
Yellow Hair, Mary 56
Yellow Hair's Brother-in-Law 56
Yellow Horse #1 56
Yellow Horse Begay 56
Yellow Horse's Daughter 56
Yellow Horse's Daughter #1 56
Yellow Horse's Grand-daughter 57
Yellow Horse's Grand-son 57

Yellow Horse's Son 57
Yellow Horse's Son #1 57
Yellow Horse's Wife 56
Yetas Bah 56
Yeth Na Do Ne 51
Yeth Ne Li Wood 51
Yinasban 18
Yith 49
Yo Cuh Ne Bah 58
Yo Des Bah 8
Yo En Tellie Bega, Hosteen 57
Yo En Tilli Hosteen, Wife 57
Yo En Tillie, Wilson 58
Yo He, Woody 33
Yo Unso 58
Yo Unso Bema 58
Ysuenthe Beta, Hosteen 58
Yus Bah 58

Za Chi Bah 57
Za He 45
Zah Bah, Ruth 35
Zah Bahhe 48
Zah Bema 41
Zah Chee 33
Zah Gey, Nellie 38
Zah Ha 10
Zah Ha Banna 10
Zah Nez Socie Beda 58
Zah Nez Soice Bega 58
Zah Sice He 16
Zah Six 1
Zah Yazzie 13
Zah, Henry 57
Zahn 11,21,23,48
Zahn Ah See 29
Zahn Chee 65
Zahn Chene 58
Zahn Chene Begay 58
Zahn Chene Bema 58
Zahn Eh He 12
Zahn Gray, Rosaline 57
Zahn Guy 5,45
Zahn Kai 28,62
Zahn Kili, Madge 31
Zahn Nezzie 20
Zahn Nie 21

Index

Zahn Nie Bah 55
Zahn Nie See He 29
Zahn Nue Bahhe 29
Zahn Se He 33
Zahn Socie 7,22
Zahn Socie, Jo Ann 25
Zahn Socie, Mary 9
Zahn Soi 9,25,50
Zahn Ta Lea 23
Zahne Bah 12
Zahne, Genevieve 21
Zahnie Goy 26
Zahnnie 33
Zahns Bahhe 7
Zahns Dahs 58
Zahns Guy 44,47
Zahns Gy Bega 58
Zahns Soi 31,39
Zan 42
Zan Nez Clanny 67
Zan Se He 45
Zan Si Benna 10
Zani 5,18,25
Zani Bahhe 35
Zani Guy 55
Zani Se He 5
Zani Se He, Mary 67
Zani Si He 25
Zani Yazze 17,53
Zani, Bah 58
Zannie 19,43
Zannie Bahhe 16
Zannie Benna 19
Zannie Jinnie Socie, Betsie 57
Zannie Tolea 51
Zannie Yazza 6,7
Zanto, Bessie 48
Ze La Bah, Gordon 49
Ze Le Soi 9
Ze Na Jinny 58
Ze Nez 25
Zed Dah So Ahloni Bitsi 43
Zedoso Howbiz 13
Zenah Bah Aszan 58
Zenah Bay Bitsey 58
Zenah Va He, Joe John 58
Zennie Soice 38

Zhuni 60
Zi Si Si 18
Zinco 22
Zinni Jinny Bega 58
Zinny Bay Aszan 34
Zinny, Aszan 59
Zith Clah Ne 59
Zoe 7
Zohn Guy 34
Zoni 53
Zoni Kay Jenny, Susie Hazel 68
Zoni Kay Kenny 59
Zoni Soi 42
Zoni Yazze 34
Zonni 68
Zonnie 21,33,47
Zuni Jinney Bah Aszan 59
Zuni Jinney Begay 59
Zuni Jinney Sonni Bitsi 60
Zuni Jinny 60
Zuni Jinny Badone 60
Zuni Jinny Sonni 60
Zuni Jinny Sonni's Wife 60
Zuni Jinny Soue 60
Zuni, Jinney 59
Zuni's, Jinney, Wife 59

www.ingramcontent.com/pod-product-compliance
Lightning Source LLC
Chambersburg PA
CBHW020300030426
42336CB00010B/844